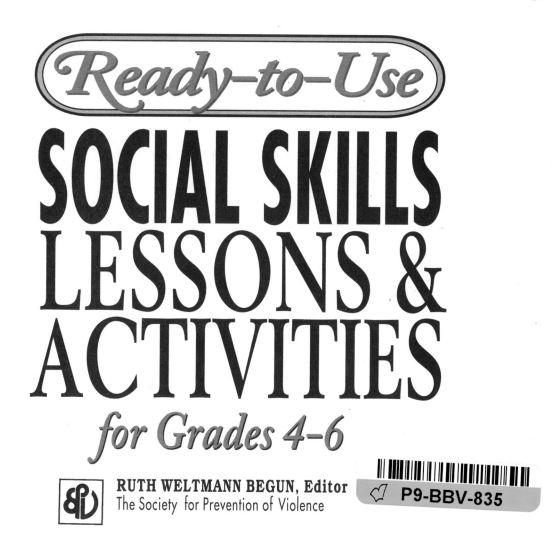

Ready-to-Use
SOCIAL SKILLS LESSONS & ACTIVITIES
for Grades 4-6

RUTH WELTMANN BEGUN, Editor
The Society for Prevention of Violence

A ready-to-use curriculum based on real-life situations to help you build children's self-esteem, self-control, respect for the rights of others, and a sense of responsibility for one's own actions.

JOSSEY-BASS
A Wiley Imprint
www.josseybass.com

Published by Jossey-Bass
A Wiley Imprint
989 Market Street, San Francisco, CA 94103-1741   www.josseybass.com

Jossey-Bass books and products are available through most bookstores. To contact Jossey-Bass
directly call our Customer Care Department within the U.S. at (800) 956-7739, outside the U.S.
at (317) 572-3986 or fax (317) 572-4002.

Jossey-Bass also publishes its books in a variety of electronic formats. Some content that appears
in print may not be available in electronic books.

Library of Congress Cataloging-in-Publication Data:
Ready-to-use social skills lessons & activities for grades 4–6
    Ruth Weltmann Begun, editor.
      p. cm.—(Social skills curriculum activities library)
    Includes bibliographical references.
    ISBN 0-87628-865-4 (Spiral)   ISBN 0-87628-474-8 (Paper)
    1. Social skills—Study and teaching. 2. Education,
Elementary—Activity programs. 3. Behavior modification. I.
Begun, Ruth Weltmann. II. Series.
LB1139.S6R43 1996   96-5194
646.7'071—dc20   CIP

Printed in the United States of America
FIRST EDITION
PB Printing 15   14   13   12   11

ABOUT THIS SOCIAL SKILLS TEACHING RESOURCE

Today's educators carry added responsibilities because significant social changes have had an impact on human relations. Family ties have been loosened. The number of single-parent families has grown. Stresses in many families are often high. Thus, youngsters are frequently exposed to influences which tend to make them aggressive and possibly violent. Moreover, television, now in almost every home, frequently shows events not suitable for guiding children. Youngsters who cannot read and write watch violent scenes and might draw wrong conclusions. Unless schools, daycare centers, head start programs, and parents counteract asocial influences starting at the pre-kindergarten level, verbal and physical interpersonal abuse and violence will be an increasing problem.

This resource is one of four books in the "Social Skills Curriculum Activities Library," a practical series designed to help teachers, care givers and parents in giving children regular social skills lessons. The full Library spans all grade levels. preschool through grade 12, and includes:

Ready-to-Use Social Skills Lessons & Activities for Grades PreK-K

Ready-to-Use Social Skills Lessons & Activities for Grades 1-3

Ready-to-Use Social Skills Lessons & Activities for Grades 4-6

Ready-to-Use Social Skills Lessons & Activities for Grades 7-12

Each grade-level book provides 50 or more detailed, age-appropriate lessons for developing specific social skills accompanied by reproducible activity sheets and other activities to help students learn the skill. The lessons are presented in a uniform format and follow a Structured Learning approach to teach the skills. They focus on real situations in children's own lives, such as dealing with feelings and peer pressure, and are readily adapted for use in any classroom, school, or home setting.

The lessons and activities in Books one, two, and three are followed by two special sections entitled "Social Skills Task Review" and "Social Skills Family Training Booklet." "Social Skills Task Review" presents 27 social skills topics that can be used for teacher-led discussions during Circle Time. These are printed in the form of discussion cards which can be photocopied and cut out for use at the appropriate time. You can introduce each topic once before studying a skill and later, following the lesson, to measure what children have learned. The Social Skills Family Training Booklet is addressed to parents and single pages can be copied as needed for use with individual children. The booklet includes a brief introduction to its purposes and acknowledgment to its originators followed by a family social skills checklist, and helpful hints and reminders for using the booklet and teaching social skills effectively. The heart of the booklet is comprised of "Fourteen Selected Social Skills" with suggested skill activities that can be done within the family.

NOTE: Copies of the booklet can be ordered from the publisher, The Center for Applied Research in Education, at the minimum quantity of 20.

Most of the lessons and activities in the Social Skills Library were written, edited, and classroom-tested by teachers from the Cleveland (Ohio) Public Schools in cooperation with faculty from John Carroll University's Department of Education. The project was funded by The Society for Prevention of Violence (SPV), a non-profit organization founded by S.J. Begun, Ph.D., and his wife Ruth Weltmann Begun, M.S., and sponsored by them and various contributing corporations and foundations. Many individual members of the SPV also made substantial contributions. Specific credits are given on the Acknowledgments page.

About This Social Skills Teaching Resource

Major objectives of teaching these lessons are to build students' self-esteem, self-control, respect for the rights of others, and a sense of responsibility for one's own actions. Another objective is to teach the students to settle grievances and conflicts through communication without recourse to violence. We believe that such training can be effective and successful by increasing discipline and reducing the drop-out rate. Thus, students will benefit from social skills training throughout their lives.

S.J. Begun, Ph.D.
Ruth Weltmann Begun, M.S.
The Society for Prevention of Violence

ACKNOWLEDGMENTS

The Founders, Trustees, Members, Friends of the Society for Prevention of Violence (SPV), and many foundations and corporations sponsored the writing of the social skills training material in the "Social Skills Curriculum Activities Library" with the objectives of reducing interpersonal violence and solving controversies in an amicable way.

Credit for writing the Grades 4–6 lessons and activities in Volume 3 in the Library belongs to a collective effort by a group of teachers and administrators of the Cleveland (Ohio) Public Schools who had unique experience in teaching children in these grade levels. They wrote under the direction of four professors from the Department of Education of the John Carroll University in Cleveland, Ohio, assisted by consultants of the Society for Prevention of Violence (SPV). The concept of a curriculum was initiated by the then Executive Director of SPV, Ruth Weltmann Begun, who did the final page collection and editing of the finished manuscripts for the Curriculum.

ABOUT THE SOCIETY FOR PREVENTION OF VIOLENCE (SPV)

The Society for Prevention of Violence (SPV) is dedicated to reducing the prevalence of violent acts and asocial behaviors in children and adults through education. It accomplishes this mission by teaching children and adults the use of the skills necessary to build their character, helping them acquire a strong values system, motivating them to develop their communication skills and to realize growth in interpersonal relationships. The mission includes integration of social and academic skills to encourage those who use them to reach their full potential and contribute to our nation's society by being able to make decisions and solve problems through effective and appropriate means.

As a non-profit organization, the Society had its origin in 1972 as The Begun Institute for The Study of Violence and Aggression at John Carroll University (Cleveland, Ohio). A multitude of information was gathered, studied, and analyzed during the ensuing ten-year period. Symposia were held which involved numerous well-known presenters and participants from various career fields. Early on, the founders of the Institute, S.J. and Ruth Begun, foresaw the trend of increasing violence in our families, communities, and across the nation, and chose to take a leadership role in pioneering an educational approach to help alleviate aggressive and antisocial behavior. The educational approach was and continues to be the sole PROACTIVE means to change behaviors. Current conditions reflect our society's reliance on reactive means of dealing with this problem. During the next ten-year period, through the determination and hard work of Ruth Weltmann Begun as executive director, the workshops, parent training sessions, collaborative projects, and a comprehensive (preschool through grade 12) Social Skills Training Curriculum were developed.

Today, classroom teachers in numerous school districts across the country are utilizing this internationally recognized curriculum. The Society continually seeks support through individual donors, grants, direct paid services, and material/consultant service sales. It also has expanded its involvement in the educational process by:

- publishing a semiannual newsletter and other pertinent articles;

- providing in-service training for professional staffs, parents, and others;

- providing assistance in resource identification, proposal writing/project design and evaluation;

- tailoring instructional (academic and other) delivery designs to specific school/organization needs; and

- implementing pilot demonstration projects with foundation support.

As we move into and through the twenty-first century, we must work diligently and cooperatively to turn challenges into success.

The Society also offers graduate-level workshops in cooperation with John Carroll University for educators. Credits earned in these workshops may be applied toward renewal of certificates through the Ohio Department of Education.

For further information, contact The Society for Prevention of Violence, 3439 West Brainard Road #102, Woodmere, Ohio 44122 (phone 216/591-1876) or 3109 Mayfield Road, Cleveland Heights, Ohio 44118 (phone 216/371-5545).

ABOUT THE SOCIAL SKILLS CURRICULUM

Philosophy

We believe that the learning of social skills is the foundation for social and academic adequacy. It assists in the prevention of social problems and leads to successful functioning and survival skills for our citizens. Social behavior and academic behavior are highly correlated. We believe it is more productive to teach children the proper ways to behave than to admonish them for improper behavior. This requires direct and systematic teaching, taking into consideration social and developmental theory in the affective, cognitive, and psycho-motor domains. Learning should be sequential, linked to community goals, and consistent with behaviors which are relevant to student needs. This social skills curriculum is based on these beliefs.

Curriculum Overview

As children grow, one way they learn social behaviors is by watching and interacting with other people. Some children who have failed to learn appropriate behaviors have lacked opportunities to imitate good role models, have received insufficient or inappropriate reinforcement, or have misunderstood adequate social experiences.

The Social Skills Curriculum is designed to teach these behaviors in ways that correlate with child development theory, namely how children learn in their natural environment. Each lesson provides models for children to imitate and correction strategies following practice of the skills. The teacher and the rest of the class then provide positive reinforcement to encourage the continued use of the appropriate skills in situations that occur in any environment.

Teachers using this curriculum can be flexible. The curriculum is designed to be used in the classroom as lessons taught for about 20–30 minutes, two to three times a week. However, it is not the intent that these be the only times social skills are taught and learned. Every opportunity should be used to reinforce, model, and coach the children so that they can practice the skills enough to feel comfortable with them as part of their ways of behaving. Therefore, the teacher should remind the students of the skills and the need to use them in all appropriate situations once the skills have been demonstrated. The teacher should also plan to model the skills in any and all interactions with the children. The teacher should be *consistent* in not only using the skills when they are taught, but in using them in all interactions with the students. Only this kind of consistent modeling will assure that the children will see the skills used repeatedly and begin to know and feel comfortable with using them. Teachers should also feel free to adapt the material to class needs and to design and develop strategies, models, and interventions other than those suggested here. Students can even be involved in helping to think of modeling strategies and other techniques.

The Social Skills Curriculum Library is graded pre-Kindergarten through Grade Twelve and presented in four volumes focusing on four different levels: grades preK–K, 1–3, 4–6, and 7–12. It uses a structured learning approach to teach the skills. *Structured Learning* is a holistic teaching method that provides a framework for systematic teaching in a way that is similar to academics. The emphasis in this curriculum is to provide constructive and structured behaviors for socially skill-deficient children.

Structured Learning consists of *four basic components:* modeling, role playing, discussion of performance, and use in real-life situations. For more effective teaching, the lessons include eight steps that follow a directed lesson format (see below):

Social Skill: A social behavior that is directly observable.

Behavioral Objective: An expected outcome of learning the social skill that can be evaluated.

Directed Lesson: Each behavior is defined and stated in observable terms; the behavior is demonstrated and practiced; a student's level of performance is evaluated and inappropriate behaviors are corrected. Positive reinforcement is used to encourage continued use of the skill in all areas of the student's environment.

1. *Establish the Need:* The purpose of teaching the lesson is included. What benefits will learning the skill provide? What are the consequences of not learning the behavior?

2. *Inroduction:* Stories, poems, puppets, and questions are used to make the social skill more concrete to the children.

3. *Identify the Skill Components:* These skill steps are used to teach the behavior. By following and practicing these steps, the students will be able to demonstrate the behavior when needed.

4. *Model the Skill:* The teacher or socially adept child demonstrates the appropriate behaviors so that the students can imitate them. The skill components are referred to during the modeling.

5. *Behavioral Rehearsal:* The children are given an opportunity to perform the behavior which can be evaluated, corrected, and reinforced.

   A. *Selection*—The teacher selects participants or asks for volunteers. The number of children depends on the time allowed and whatever is appropriate for each lesson.

   B. *Role Play*—The participants are assigned their roles or situations they will role play.

   C. *Completion*—This is a means to determine that the role playing is complete. After each role play, reinforce correct behaviors, identify inappropriate behaviors, and reenact role play with corrections. If there are no corrections, role play is complete.

   D. *Reinforcers*—Positive reinforcement by the teacher and the class is used for maintenance of the skill. Various methods can be used: verbal encouragement, tangible rewards, special privileges, and keeping a record of social and academic improvement.

   E. *Discussion*—The student's level of performance is evaluated and inappropriate behaviors are corrected. How did the participants feel while performing? What difficulties might be faced in implementing the skill? What observations did the class make?

6. *Practice:* Activities that help the children summarize the skill. The practice can be done by using worksheets, doing art projects, making film strips, writing stories, keeping diaries and charts, and so on.

7. *Independent Use:* Activities that help facilitate the use of these behaviors outside the school environment. Family and friends take an active role in reinforcing the importance of using these alternative behaviors in a conflict situation.

8. *Continuation:* At the end of each lesson, the teacher reminds the class that applying social skills can benefit them in academic and social relationships. Stress that, although there are difficulties in applying the skills (such as in regard to negative peer pressure), the benefits outweigh the problems. One such benefit is more self-confidence in decision making. Maintaining social behavior is an ongoing process. It requires teachers to show appropriate behaviors and reinforce them when they are demonstrated.

STRUCTURED LEARNING
4 Basic Components

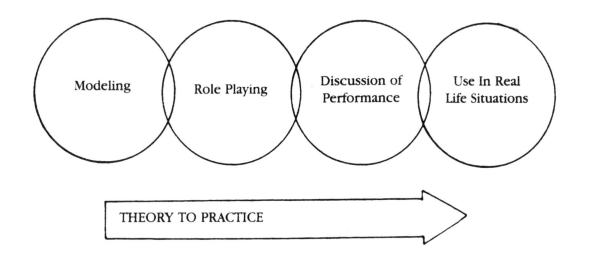

Modeling · Role Playing · Discussion of Performance · Use In Real Life Situations

THEORY TO PRACTICE

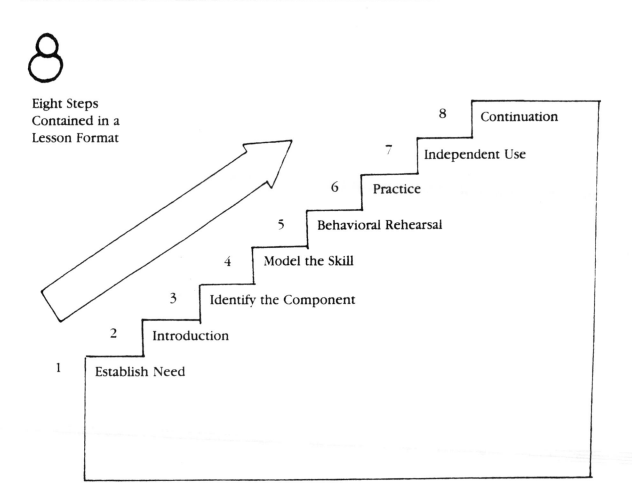

Eight Steps
Contained in a
Lesson Format

1 Establish Need
2 Introduction
3 Identify the Component
4 Model the Skill
5 Behavioral Rehearsal
6 Practice
7 Independent Use
8 Continuation

BIBLIOGRAPHY

Books

Apter, Stephen J., and Arnold P. Goldstein. *Youth Violence: Program and Prospects.* Needham Heights, MA: Allyn & Bacon, 1986.

Ballare, Antonia, and Angelique Lampros. *Behavior Smart! Ready-to-Use Activities for Building Personal and Social Skills for Grades K–4.* West Nyack, NY: Center for Applied Research in Education, 1994.

Cartledge, Gwendolyn, and Joanne Fellows Milburn. *Teaching Social Skills to Children,* 2nd ed. Needham Heights, MA: Allyn & Bacon, 1986.

Cherry, Clare. *Please Don't Sit on the Kids: Alternatives to Punitive Discipline.* Belmont, CA: Fearon-Pitman, 1982.

Chirinian, Helene. *Cartoon Comprehension.* Redondo Beach, CA: Frank Schaeffer Publications, 1980.

Eberle, Bob. *Help! in Managing Your Classroom.* Carthage, IL: Good Apple, 1984.

Farnette, C., I Forte, and B. Loss. *I've Got Me and I'm Glad,* rev. ed. Nashville, TN: Incentive Publications, 1989.

Feshbach, Norma, and Seymour Feshback et al. *Learning to Care: Classroom Activities for Social and Affective Development.* Glenview, IL: Good Year Books, 1983.

Ginott, Haim G. *Teacher and Child: A Book for Parents.* New York: Macmillan, 1984.

Goldstein, Arnold P., Stephen J. Apter, and Berj Harootunian. *School Violence.* Englewood Cliffs, NJ: Prentice Hall, 1984.

Goldstein, Arnold P. et al. *Skillstreaming the Adolescent: A Structured Learning Approach to Teaching Prosocial Skills.* Champaign, IL: Research Press, 1980.

Grevious, Saundrah Clark. *Ready-to-Use Multicultural Activities for Primary Children.* West Nyack, NY: Center for Applied Research in Education, 1993.

Kaplan, P.G., S.K. Crawford, and S.L. Nelson. *Nice.* Denver: Love, 1977.

Mannix, Darlene. *Be a Better Student: Lessons and Worksheets for Teaching Behavior Management in Grades 4–9.* West Nyack, NY: Center for Applied Research in Education, 1989.

_____. *Life Skills Activities for Special Children.* West Nyack, NY: Center for Applied Research in Education, 1991.

_____. *Social Skills Activities for Special Children.* West Nyack, NY: Center for Applied Research in Education, 1993.

McElmurry, Mary Ann. *Caring.* Carthage, IL: Good Apple, 1981.

_____. *Feelings.* Carthage, IL: Good Apple, 1981.

McGinnis, Ellen, and Arnold P. Goldstein. *Skillstreaming the Elementary School Child: A Guide for Teaching Prosocial Skills.* Champaign, IL: Research Press, 1984.

Schwartz, Linda. *The Month-to-Month Me.* Santa Barbara, CA: The Learning Works, 1976.

Standish, Bob. *Connecting Rainbows.* Carthage, IL: Good Apple, 1982.

Stephens, Thomas M. *Social Skills in the Classroom,* 2nd ed. Lutz, FL: Psychological Assessment Resources, 1992.

Stull, Elizabeth Crosby. *Multicultural Discovery Activities for the Elementary Grades.* West Nyack, NY: Center for Applied Research in Education, 1994.

Teolis, Beth. *Ready-to-Use Self-Esteem & Conflict-Solving Activities for Grades 4–8.* West Nyack, NY: Center for Applied Research in Education, 1995.

Toner, Patricia Rizzo. *Relationships & Communication Activities.* West Nyack, NY: Center for Applied Research in Education, 1993.

_____. *Stress Management & Self-Esteem Activities.* West Nyack, NY: Center for Applied Research in Education, 1993.

Documents

Early Identification of Classification of Juvenile Delinquents: Hearing Before the Subcommittee of the Committee on the Constitution, U.S. Senate, 97th Congress; Serial No. J-97-70; October 22, 1981; Testimony by: Gerald R. Patterson, Research Scientist—Oregon Social Learning Center, Eugene, Oregon; David Farrington and John Monahan.

Ounces of Prevention: Toward an Understanding of the Causes of Violence; by State of California Commission on Crime Control and Violence Prevention, 1982.

CONTENTS

About This Social Skills Teaching Resource iii

Acknowledgments v

About the Society for Prevention of Violence (SPV) vi

About the Social Skills Curriculum vii

Bibliography x

SOCIAL SKILLS LESSONS & ACTIVITIES FOR GRADES 4-6

Lesson *Social Skill* *Page*

DISCIPLINARY STRATEGIES

1 LEARNING APPROPRIATE AND CONTROLLED BEHAVIOR 1
   Reproducible Contract
                   "Appropriate Actions" Activity Sheet

2 RECOGNIZING THE NEED FOR RULES/CONSEQUENCES 5
   Reproducible "Rules and Consequences" Activity Sheet
                   "Violations and Penalties" Activity Sheet

3 ACCEPTING APPROPRIATE DISCIPLINARY ACTIONS .9
   Reproducible Personal Record Sheet
                   Contract

THINKING BEFORE ACTING

4 FULLY UNDERSTANDING THE SITUATION BEFORE TAKING ACTION 13
   Reproducible "What's Happening?" Activity Sheet
                   "A Detective Story" Activity Sheet

5 GETTING ALL THE FACTS BEFORE ACTING 17
   Reproducible "Understand the Situation" Activity Sheet
                   "Family Interview" Activity Sheet

6 AVOIDING THOUGHTLESS ACTIONS 21
   Reproducible "Scrambled Words" Activity Sheet
                   "Sentence Sense" Activity Sheet

LISTENING

7 BEING A GOOD LISTENER 25
   Reproducible "Listen to Learn" Activity Sheet

8 FOLLOWING VERBAL DIRECTIONS 28
   Reproducible "A Lesson Was Learned" Activity Sheet

9 ABILITY TO SIT AND LISTEN QUIETLY 31
   Reproducible "Find a Good Listener" Game
                   Good Listener Chart

Contents

10 PARAPHRASING WHAT IS HEARD 35
Reproducible "Listening Survey" Activity Sheet
"My Best Listening" Activity Sheet

11 ABILITY TO LISTEN/PARTICIPATE IN CLASS DISCUSSION 39
Reproducible "Listening" Activity Sheet

12 ATTENDING TO THE SPEAKER 42
Reproducible "How Good Are You at Following Directions?" Exercise Sheet
"Who's a Good Listener" Activity Sheet

FOLLOWING INSTRUCTIONS

13 FOLLOWING SPECIFIC INSTRUCTIONS 46
Reproducible "Where Are You Now?" Activity Sheet
Verbal Instructions for Following Map

14 ABILITY TO FOLLOW VERBAL DIRECTIONS 50

IMPROVING SELF-IMAGE

15 FEELING GOOD ABOUT ONESELF 52
Reproducible "Toot Your Own Horn!" Activity Sheet
"Things We Do Well" Activity Sheet

16 HELPING ANOTHER PERSON 55
Reproducible "Blue Ribbon" Activity Sheet

17 KNOWING YOURSELF 58
Reproducible "Knowing Myself" Activity Sheet
"Things I Do Well" Activity Sheet

18 RECOGNIZING YOUR STRENGTHS AND WEAKNESSES 62
Reproducible "Two Great Men" Activity Sheet
"Things I Need to Improve" Activity Sheet

19 UNDERSTANDING OUR UNIQUENESS 66

20 RECOGNIZING ONE'S SPECIAL QUALITY 68
Reproducible "My Best Trait" Activity Sheet

ACCEPTING CONSEQUENCES

21 ACCEPTING THE CONSEQUENCES FOR BREAKING THE RULES 71
Reproducible "Choosing a Consequence" Activity Sheet

22 ACCEPTING THE CONSEQUENCES FOR INAPPROPRIATE BEHAVIOR 74
Reproducible "Truth and Consequence" Activity Sheet

23 ACCEPTING CONSEQUENCES WITHOUT ANGER 77
Reproducible "Tell the Truth Interview" Activity Sheet

24   RESPONDING CALMLY TO FAILURE 80
     Reproducible   "What Is Failure?" Activity Sheet

25   ACCEPTING CONSEQUENCES FOR INAPPROPRIATE BEHAVIOR 83
     Reproducible   "Write the Consequence" Activity Sheet
                      "Letter to Home" Activity Sheet

26 USING PROBLEM-SOLVING SKILLS 87
     Reproducible   "Consequences of Behavior" Activity Sheet
                      "Problem Solving" Activity Sheet

USING SELF-CONTROL

27   REFUSING REQUESTS IN A POSITIVE MANNER 91

28   APPLYING DECISION-MAKING SKILLS 93
     Reproducible   "What's Your Reaction?" Activity Sheet
                      "Reaction Sheet"

29   MAINTAINING SELF-CONTROL 97
     Reproducible   "Self-Control Reaction Sheet" Activity Sheet

30   REMAINING CALM UNDER STRESS 100
     Reproducible   "A Trying Situation" Activity Sheet

31   PRACTICING SELF-RESTRAINT 103

GOAL SETTING

32   LEARNING TO SET A GOAL 105

33   SETTING SUCCESSIVE GOALS 107
     Reproducible   "Setting Goals" Activity Sheet
                      "Weekly Goals Chart" Activity Sheet

34   SETTING AND ACHIEVING GOALS 111

COMPLETING ASSIGNMENTS

35   FINISHING TASKS ON TIME 113
     Reproducible   "On Task" Activity Sheet
                      "Completing Assignments" Activity Sheet

36   AN ASSIGNED TASK 117
     Reproducible   "Completing Assignments" Activity Sheet

37   FINISHING ASSIGNMENTS ON TIME 120
     Reproducible   "Completing Assignment Cartoon" Activity Sheet
                      "Completing Assignment Chart" Activity Sheet

38   WORKING TO COMPLETE ASSIGNMENTS 124
     Reproducible   "The Completed Assignment" Award Sheet

Contents

PROBLEM SOLVING

39 LISTING PROBLEM-SOLVING STEPS 127
    Reproducible   "You Be the Judge" Activity Sheet

40 MAKING A DECISION 130
    Reproducible   "Decisions, Decisions!" Activity Sheet

41 REVIEWING PROBLEM-SOLVING CHOICES 133
    Reproducible   "The Interview" Activity Sheet
                     "Transfer Activity" Activity Sheet

42 MANAGING CONFLICT 137
    Reproducible   "Malcolm's Conflict" Activity Sheet
                     "Decision Time" Activity Sheet

43 APPLYING A METHOD TO SOLVE PROBLEMS .141
    Reproducible   "Sherlock Hound" Puppet

44 USING A PLAN TO SOLVE PROBLEMS 144
    Reproducible   "My Plan" Activity Sheet

DEALING WITH ANGER

45 COMMUNICATING ANGER WITH WORDS 147
    Reproducible   "Poster Art" Activity Sheet

46 CONTROLLING ONE'S ANGER 150
    Reproducible   "What Should You Do? Activity Sheet

47 USING SELF-CONTROL STEPS 154
    Reproducible   "Sorting Out Anger" Activity Sheet

48 USING SELF-CONTROL STEPS 157
    Reproducible   "Resolving Anger" Activity Sheet
                     "A Conflict Taken From History" Activity Sheet

49 RECOGNIZING WORDS THAT SPARK ANGER 161
    Reproducible   "Trigger Words and Personal Identity" Activity Sheet

50 RECOGNIZING ANOTHER'S ANGER 164
    Reproducible   "Understanding Another Person's Anger" Activity Sheet

ACCEPTING CHANGE

51 ACCEPTING GOOD OR BAD CHANGES 167
    Reproducible   "Changes Collage" Activity Sheet
                     "Changes at Home" Activity Sheet

52 REACTING TO CHANGE 171
    Reproducible   "Changes From Life in a Skyscraper to Life in a Farmhouse"
                     Activity Sheet
                     "Survey Sheet"

53   ADJUSTING TO CHANGE 175
      Reproducible   Crossword Puzzle
                   "My Reactions to Change" Activity Sheet

DEALING WITH FEELINGS

54   SHOWING THAT WE CARE 179
      Reproducible   "How Would You Feel?" Activity Sheet

55   DEMONSTRATING SPORTSMANSHIP 182
      Reproducible   "Sportsmanship" Activity Sheet

56   RECOGNIZING ANOTHER'S EMOTIONS 185
      Reproducible   "What Emotions Do You See?" Activity Sheet

57   RESPECTING OTHERS' VIEWPOINTS 188
      Reproducible   "Two Viewpoints" Activity Sheet

58   APOLOGIZING WHEN AT FAULT 191
      Reproducible   "How to Apologize" Activity Sheet

59   COMPLIMENTING OTHERS 194
      Reproducible   "Understanding Feelings" Activity Sheet

60   PRACTICING ACTIVE LISTENING 197
      Reproducible   "Observer's Chart: Active Listening Behavior"
                   Activity Sheet

61   IDENTIFYING EMOTIONAL TONES 200

62   EXPRESSING UNDERSTANDING 202
      Reproducible   "What Are They Feeling?" Activity Sheet

DEALING WITH PREJUDICE

63   RECOGNIZING INDIVIDUAL DIFFERENCES 205
      Reproducible   "Word Search" Activity Sheet
                   "Different Times" Activity Sheet

64   ACCEPTING EACH PERSON'S UNIQUENESS 209
      Reproducible   "Dealing With Prejudices" Activity Sheet
                   "The Aliens Have Landed!" Activity Sheet

65   APPRECIATING OUR DIFFERENCES 213
      Reproducible   "Treasure Hunt" Activity Sheet
                   "Positive Qualities" Activity Sheet

DEALING WITH PEER PRESSURE

66   SAYING "NO" TO NEGATIVE PEER PRESSURE 217
      Reproducible   "What's Your Decision?" Activity Sheet

Contents

67 IGNORING PEER PRESSURE 220
    Reproducible   The Answer Is "No" Activity Sheet

68 SAYING "NO" TO NEGATIVE GROUP PRESSURE 223
    Reproducible   "John's Dilemma" Activity Sheet
                     "Lunchroom Survey" Activity Sheet

69 RESISTING NEGATIVE PEER PRESSURE 227
    Reproducible   "Handling Peer Pressure" Activity Sheet

70 KNOWING YOUR OWN UNIQUE QUALITIES 230
    Reproducible   "I'm Unique" Activity Sheet
                     "Summary of The Sneetches by Dr. Seuss" Activity Sheet

71 LEARNING TO THINK INDEPENDENTLY 234
    Reproducible   "Peer-Pressure Situations" Activity Sheet

    STOPPING FALSE RUMORS

72 PREVENTING THE SPREAD OF RUMORS 237
    Reproducible   "Stopping a Rumor" Activity Sheet
                     "Don't Spread Rumors" Activity Sheet

73 PREVENTING FALSE RUMORS 241
    Reproducible   "Stopping False Rumors" Activity Sheet
                     "Rumor Busters Interview" Activity Sheet

74 PREVENTING SPREADING OF FALSE RUMORS 245
    Reproducible   "Telephone" Activity Sheet
                     "Rumor Doomer Badge" Activity Sheet

SOCIAL SKILLS TASK REVIEW

Part I: Topics for Class Discussions on Reproducible Discussion Cards 249
Part II: Review of Social Skills 259
Transparency Master "Something to Tackle" 260

SOCIAL SKILLS FAMILY TRAINING BOOKLET

Introduction and "Family Letter" (reproducible) 261

"PARTNERS IN SOCIAL SKILLS: A FAMILY AFFAIR"

(Single Pages Reproducible as Marked)

1   Cover Page

2   Copyright and Acknowledgments

3   Introduction

4   Table of Contents (reproducible pages are marked)

5   Our Family Social Skills Training Checklist

6   Helpful Hints for Using This Book

7   Be a Role Model for Your Child

8   Family Activity Page

9   Fourteen Selected Social Skills With Suggested Activities

    Skill No. 1   Giving Compliments

    Skill No. 2   Asking Permission

    Skill No. 3   Disciplinary Strategies

    Skill No. 4   Respect for Others

    Skill No. 5   Using Self-Control

    Skill No. 6   Improving Self-Image

    Skill No. 7   Expressing Feelings

    Skill No. 8   Accepting Consequences

    Skill No. 9   Reacting to Failure

    Skill No. 10   Setting Goals

    Skill No. 11   Dealing With Prejudice

    Skill No. 12   Dealing With Anger

    Skill No. 13   Dealing With Peer Pressure

    Skill No. 14   Problem Solving

17   Family Activity Page

18   "Mirror, Mirror" Poem

19   Family Activity Page, Certificate

20   Family Time—Group Discussions

21   What Makes You Happy?

22   Parent-Teacher Communication

23   Our Family Social Skills Training Checklist

24   Guidelines for Caring Parents

SOCIAL SKILLS LESSONS & ACTIVITIES FOR GRADES 4-6
To the Teacher

The following pages present 74 ready-to-use social skills lessons with a variety of related activities and worksheets. All of the lessons have been tested and are suggested for use with students in the elementary (4–6) grades.

The lessons may be used in any order you desire, though they are sequenced in a general way, beginning with disciplinary strategies for the classroom. Ultimately, of course, you will match the needs and ability levels of your pupils with the particular lessons and social skills learning objectives. Some of the lessons may have to be repeated several times over the course of the school year.

You may want to introduce a social skill in class discussion before presenting the related lesson, as suggested in the "Social Skills Task Review" on page 249 . This should give you an idea of how familiar children may or may not be with the skill. The skill can then be discussed by the class again following the lesson to see how many children have learned this skill.

The patterns and activity sheets accompanying these lessons may be photocopied as many times as you need them for use with individual children, small groups, or the whole class. You may also devise activity sheets of your own to enrich and reinforce any of the lessons.

SOCIAL SKILL
Learning Appropriate and Controlled Behavior

Behavioral Objective: The student will learn appropriate and controlled behavior in order to promote a positive classroom environment.

Directed Lesson:

1. **Establish the Need:** The teacher will point out the need to establish appropriate and sometimes disciplinary action when necessary by taking away or adding activities that the student enjoys to ensure a peaceful classroom environment.

2. **Introduction:** The teacher will ask the class:

    1. **"Can we do whatever we want, when we want?"**
    2. **"What would happen if there were no rules for the lunchroom, the classroom, your home, or street traffic?"**
    3. **Why are rules important?"**

   Teacher establishes rules using the black board to list them. Students will help develop consequences to fit each broken rule.

3. **Identify the Skill Components:** Write the following skill components on the board before class.

    1. Develop rules.
    2. Develop consequences.
    3. Be positive in your actions.
    4. Recognize the need for consequences.

4. **Model the Skill:** Reverse roles. The teacher portrays a problem student, while the student portrays the teacher. Act out a situation in which the teacher behaves poorly and the student decides on an appropriate disciplinary action with discussion following from the rest of the class.

5. **Behavior Rehearsal:**

    A. **Selection:** Choose one student to act as the accused or defendant. Select twelve students to serve as jury.

    B. **Role Play:** Teacher describes a crime; for example: a student was caught stealing candy from a drugstore. Police were called and now the accused is on trial. The teacher acts as judge/mediator. The rest of the class asks questions of the accused, such as:

    1. Did you know it is illegal to steal?

1

    2. Is this your first time or have you done this before?

    3. Do you know what could happen to you for doing this?

        The jury decides on disciplinary action to be taken (e.g., community service, counseling, juvenile home, etc.) depending on whether this is a first offense (community service), second offense (counseling), or third offense (juvenile home).

  C. ***Completion:*** After each role play, reinforce correct behavior, identify inappropriate behaviors, and reenact role play with corrections. If there are no corrections, role play is complete.

  D. ***Reinforcers:*** Verbal praise, nonverbal approval (smile, pat, or hug).

  E. ***Discussion:*** Teacher and students will discuss how the court system works in real life, alternative consequences for crimes, and if the judicial system is effective as a disciplinary action.

6. ***Practice:*** Distribute copies of the following "Contract" activity sheet and have students list class rules and consequences and sign their contract.

7. ***Independent Use:*** Distribute and have students complete the "Appropriate Actions" activity sheet. Upon return of the activity sheet, use it to discuss appropriate actions. Go over the "Appropriate Action" activity sheet and "Contract" as a group.

8. ***Continuation:*** Teacher should continue pointing out the need for leaving controlled and appropriate behaviors as related situations arise.

CONTRACT

List Class Rules: _____

_____

_____

_____

_____

_____

_____

Consequences: _____

_____

_____

_____

_____

_____

_____

_____

I agree to follow these rules and accept the consequences for my actions.

Name: (Print) _____ Date: _____

Signature: _____ Date: _____

Name _____ Date _____

APPROPRIATE ACTIONS

Directions: Determine appropriate action for the following situations. Write this information under each statement.

1. You forgot your homework assignment.

   _____

   _____

   _____

2. You broke a window at your house.

   _____

   _____

   _____

3. You lost something you borrowed from a friend.

   _____

   _____

   _____

4. You lost the money your parent gave you to go to the store.

   _____

   _____

   _____

SOCIAL SKILL
Recognizing the Need for Rules/Consequences

Behavioral Objective: The student will recognize and develop disciplinary actions for inappropriate behavior. He/she will be able to avoid uncontrolled negative behavior to ensure a positive educational environment.

Directed Lesson:

1. ***Establish the Need:*** Teacher initiates a class discussion of the need for taking some form of disciplinary action when rules are broken. Rules must be enforced in order for people to live and work together, and accomplish goals in society.

2. ***Introduction:*** Using football or any other sport, the teacher discusses the consequences for violating the rules during a game. Example of questions: **"How is football played? What happens when a player runs into a kicker? What action is taken when the team is off-side? What is done about grabbing a player's face-mask when tackling? Why do they have these disciplinary actions? (For protection of the players, so that the game will be played fairly.) These are the same reasons we have disciplinary actions when a rule or law is broken."**

3. ***Identify the Skill Components:*** (List on board or place on sentence strips.)

    1. Think about the behavior.
    2. Discuss the rules (shown on board).
    3. Discuss possible disciplinary actions and consequences.
    4. Choose the most appropriate actions or consequences.

4. ***Model the Skill:*** The teacher will demonstrate a behavior where he/she breaks a rule. Have students discuss possible disciplinary strategies for the rule that is broken. (List suggestions on board.) Have the class agree on the most appropriate disciplinary action for the behavior that broke a rule.

5. ***Behavioral Rehearsal:***

    A. ***Selection:*** Teacher chooses three to four volunteer students to role play.

    B. ***Role Play:*** Have one student act as the teacher, and read a rule. Then lead class through the skill steps. (Choose a different student to lead class by referring to the rules discussed.)

    C. ***Completion:*** After each role play, reinforce correct behavior, identify inappropriate behavior, and reenact role play with corrections. If there are no corrections, role play is complete.

    D. ***Reinforcers:*** Material rewards, verbal encouragements such as "good job!," "you chose an appropriate action," etc. group encouragement.

    E. ***Discussion:*** Have students discuss the importance of enforcing rules, why the disciplinary action should be an appropriate consequence, and why consequences should be accepted.

6. ***Practice:*** Distribute copies of the activity sheet entitled "Rules and Consequences" and read through the directions with the class. After students have completed the activity sheet, discuss appropriate disciplinary actions.

7. ***Independent Use:*** Give students copies of the activity sheet entitled "Violations and Penalties." Ask them to watch a pro sports game on TV and list the violations and penalties that occur. Use the activity sheet as the basis for class discussion when it is returned.

8. ***Continuation:*** Teacher continues to point out the need for appropriate enforcement of rules in order for people to live and work together productively and peacefully.

CHILDREN'S LITERATURE

Secure a number of sports books from the library for students to learn football rules and how to play the game.

Tie in the importance of rules and teamwork within the classroom setting.

Name _____ Date _____

RULES AND CONSEQUENCES

Directions: List rules and consequences on football yard lines.

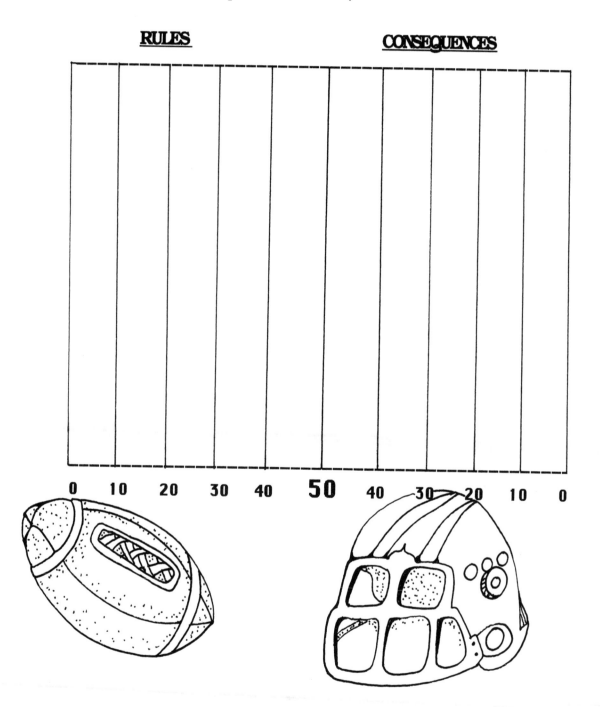

RULES **CONSEQUENCES**

0   10   20   30   40   **50**   40   30   20   10   0

Name _____ Date _____

VIOLATIONS AND PENALTIES

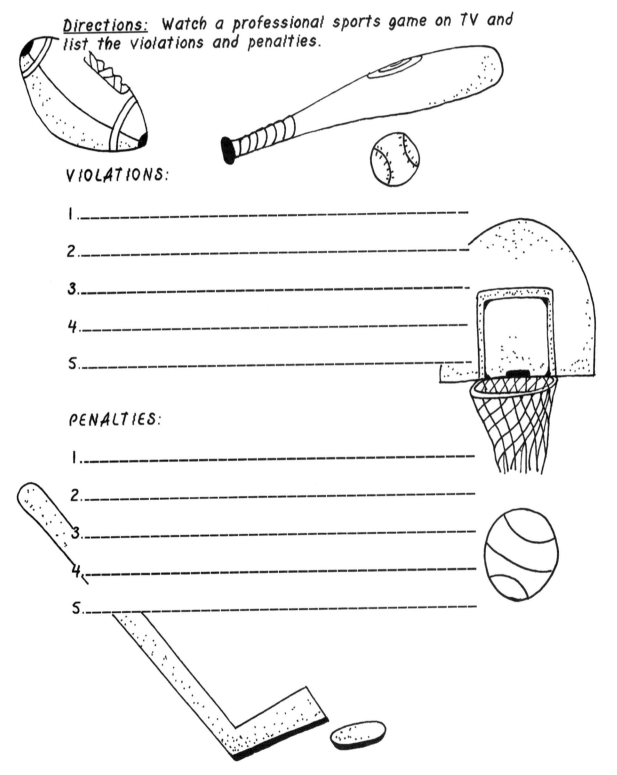

<u>Directions:</u> Watch a professional sports game on TV and list the violations and penalties.

VIOLATIONS:

1. _____

2. _____

3. _____

4. _____

5. _____

PENALTIES:

1. _____

2. _____

3. _____

4. _____

5. _____

SOCIAL SKILL

Accepting Appropriate Disciplinary Actions

Behavioral Objective: The student will be able to accept appropriate disciplinary action, and avoid uncontrolled negative behavior, to assure an environment conducive to learning and living.

Directed Lesson:

1. **Establish the Need:** The teacher points out that it is necessary to use appropriate disciplinary action and when necessary to take away or add activities which the student enjoys to ensure a productive and peaceful environment in the classroom.

2. **Introduction:** The teacher will stress that it is important to develop appropriate disciplinary actions for rules that have been transgressed. Possible consequences might include:

   1. Exclusion from optional activities
   2. Disciplinary special assignment
   3. Name on board
   4. Parents notified
   5. Referral to principal

   It is imperative that the student recognizes and accepts disciplinary actions to suit the misbehavior.

3. **Identify the Skill Components:** (List on board before class.)

   1. Follow the rules at school and at home.
   2. Think of the consequences before you act.
   3. Be prepared to accept the consequences of your behavior.
   4. Make a conscious effort to choose the behavior that will assure a positive environment.

4. **Model the Skill:** Teacher will model the skill by using the skill components in a staged situation with a student.

5. **Behavioral Rehearsal:**

   A. **Selection:** Select four pairs of students. Two pairs will role play student-teacher relationships. Two pairs will role play child-parent relationships.

   B. **Role Play:** Students will play out situations they have encountered in their own lives. They will then tell how they used the disciplinary strategies to assure a positive environment.

    C. ***Completion:*** After each role play, reinforce correct behavior, identify inappropriate behaviors, and reenact role play with corrections. If there are no corrections, role play is complete.

    D. ***Reinforcers:*** Verbal praise from teacher and peers.

    E. ***Discussion:*** Discuss the role playing and how well the students were able to control their behavior to ensure a positive environment.

6. ***Practice:*** Students will use the following "Personal Record Sheet" to evaluate themselves and their behaviors within a time given by the teacher. When the time is up, have students discuss results in class.

7. ***Independent Use:*** Each student will take the "Contract" home. He/she will explain the social skill learned at school today and how it will apply at home. This will be a contract between the parent and child to help the child accept appropriate disciplinary action when necessary, by taking away or adding activities which the student enjoys.

8. ***Continuation:*** Teachers should continue pointing out the need for appropriate rules/consequences as related situations arise.

CHILDREN'S LITERATURE

Secure a number of sports stories by Matt Christopher from the public library and encourage students to read them during silent reading time. Boys, especially, are drawn to these stories. Some of the book titles are as follows: *Baseball Flyhawk, Football Fugitive, Skateboard Tough, Johnny Long Legs,* etc.

Name _____ Date _____

PERSONAL RECORD SHEET

Situation	*Reaction*	*Consequences*

Name _____ Date _____

CONTRACT

I, _____, do promise to abide by
(student name)

the rules and regulations at home and school and to accept disci-

plinary action, when necessary, by the taking away or adding of

activities.

The purpose of this contract is to assure an environment con-

ducive to learning and living.

* *

I, _____, do accept this promise
(parent signature)

from my child.

* *

THINKING BEFORE ACTING   Lesson 4

SOCIAL SKILL
Fully Understanding the Situation Before Taking Action

Behavioral Objective: The student will find out about all the occurrences and facts that have created a situation or conflict before he/she will take action.

Directed Lesson:

1. **Establish the Need:** The purpose is to understand the reasons (both physical and psychological) of the person who created the situation so as not to attack the person but the problem.

2. **Introduction:** The teacher asks:

   "Do you like being accused of something wrong that you didn't do? How do you feel? Have you ever been wrongly accused by another person?"

   The discussion should emphasize the need of understanding the whole situation before accusing someone.

3. **Identify the Skill Components:** (List on board before class.)

   1. Observe the situation.
   2. Ask questions.
   3. Understand all aspects and facts.
   4. Analyze the situation.
   5. Make decisions.

4. **Model the Skill:** Teacher models the skill by accusing a student in the room of stealing from someone's desk. A discussion follows using the skill steps.

5. **Behavioral Rehearsal:**

   A. **Selection:** Two students are to participate in the role play.

   B. **Role Play:** The teacher gives one student prepared role play cards to read a story, and sends the other student out of the room temporarily. The first student then reads the story, for example: "Two friends were playing together in Sid's backyard. His father raised rabbits and the boys were looking at the large pens. Sid told Ted not to open the pens because the rabbits would escape. While Sid ran to the swing set, Ted opened the pens. Four rabbits jumped out. Ted ran away."

   The teacher now calls back the student sent out of the room and the story is continued.

13

"Sid jumped off the swing set and ran toward the pens. When Sid's mother came outside, she saw Sid chasing the rabbits. She said, "I thought your father made it clear to you to stay away from the rabbits' pens.""

Now the teacher asks the student who returned in the middle of the story for his opinion of the situation.

A discussion follows informing the student who was outside while all the facts were discussed, to stress the importance of learning all the facts before drawing a conclusion. Did the student's opinion change after discovering all the facts?

    C. ***Completion:*** After each role play, reinforce correct behavior, identify inappropriate behaviors, and reenact role play with corrections. If there are no corrections, role play is complete.

    D. ***Reinforcers:*** Verbal praise, nonverbal approval (smile, pat, hug).

    E. ***Discussion:*** Have students discuss the merits of investigating the situation before taking action. Ask them what experiences they have had with being wrongly accused.

6. ***Practice:*** Distribute copies of the activity sheet entitled "What's Happening?" Have students complete the activity then discuss their responses.

7. ***Independent Use:*** Give students copies of the activity sheet entitled "A Detective Story" and ask them to compose a story as a home assignment.

8. ***Continuation:*** Teacher should continue to point out the importance of getting all the facts before acting as related situations arise.

Name _____ Date _____

WHAT'S HAPPENING ?

DIRECTIONS:

PICTURE #1: If you were the child walking into this situation, write the steps you would take to determine what is happening.

1.

\- - - - - - - - - - - - - -

\- - - - - - - - - - - - - -

\- - - - - - - - - - - - - -

\- - - - - - - - - - - - - -

\- - - - - - - - - - - - - -

\- - - - - - - - - - - - - -

\- - - - - - - - - - - - - -

PICTURE #2: Write two or three sentences describing the boy's intentions. Remember to look carefully at the whole situation.

2.

\- - - - - - - - - - - - - -

\- - - - - - - - - - - - - -

\- - - - - - - - - - - - - -

\- - - - - - - - - - - - - -

\- - - - - - - - - - - - - -

\- - - - - - - - - - - - - -

\- - - - - - - - - - - - - -

Name _____ Date _____

A DETECTIVE STORY

Directions: Write a story involving a detective trying to solve a mystery. After completing your story, list the details or clues used to solve the problem.

TITLE: _____

_____

_____

_____

_____

_____

_____

_____

_____

_____

_____

_____

_____

_____

_____

_____

_____

_____

(You can use the other side too).

THINKING BEFORE ACTING

SOCIAL SKILL
Getting All the Facts Before Acting

Behavioral Objective: The student will be able to understand the total situation before taking action.

Directed Lesson:

1. ***Establish the Need:*** Teacher discusses with the class the need for totally understanding a situation by investigating all possible solutions before an action is taken. Knowing that they have chosen the most meaningful action will make them feel good about themselves.

2. ***Introduction:*** Teacher reads a detective story, where a situation is investigated before an action is taken. Teacher discusses the sequential steps in the story, then asks the class what to do next after knowing the situation. Discuss the action taken in the story.

3. ***Identify the Skill Components:*** (List on board or place on sentence strips.)

    1. Investigate the situation.
    2. Ask meaningful questions.
    3. Collect all the facts.
    4. Look at possible solutions.
    5. Decide on what action to take.
    6. Do it.
    7. Evaluate your actions.

4. ***Model the Skill:*** Teacher reads the following:

    "The class left the room to attend a program in the auditorium. Ted left the room last because he had to put some materials away. When the class returned to the room and was asked to take out their science notebooks, Sam raised his hand to complain that his notebook wasn't in his desk."

    Teacher then follows skill steps to show how the final action was decided upon. (Sample solutions: Did someone come into the room? Sam might have left it on the bus, at home, or in the coatroom. Did Ted take it? etc.).

5. ***Behavioral Rehearsal:***

    A. ***Selection:*** Teacher selects four students to role play the following incident.

    B. ***Role Play:*** One student reads the teacher's part. The other students are the pupils.

Teacher: "Someone erased what I wrote on my board while I was out of the room. Johnny, weren't you the last one in the room?" *Johnny:* "Yes, but when I left the room, the writing was still on the board."

Teacher: "Nancy, you're in charge of room chores. Did you erase the writing by mistake?" *Nancy:* "No, you told me not to erase anything on the board until tomorrow."

Sam: "Teacher, remember you told the art teacher he could use the room for his class on your free period. Maybe he did it." *Teacher:* "Yes, I did tell him that. I'll check and see if he used the board. Thanks, Sam, for reminding me."

C. **Completion:** After the role play, reinforce correct behavior, identify inappropriate behavior, and reenact role play with corrections. If no corrections, role play is complete.

D. **Reinforcers:** Verbal encouragement, group encouragement, verbal praise, material rewards.

E. **Discussion:** Students discuss other situations and possible solutions before a final action is taken. Students should then evaluate the appropriateness of that action.

6. **Practice:** Distribute copies of the activity sheet entitled "Understand the Situation," then read through the directions and story with the class. Have students complete the story applying the skill steps, then share their story completions.

7. **Independent Use:** Give students copies of the activity sheet entitled "Family Interview." Students are asked to question family member(s) about a situation where they acted before understanding the total situation. Share the results with the class one week after the activity sheet is handed out.

8. **Completion:** Teacher should continue to point out the need for knowing all the facts before acting as related situations arise.

CHILDREN'S LITERATURE

Outrageous humor and books that appeal to students are the books by Bruce Coville, which can be secured from the public library. Some titles are: *Aliens Ate My Homework, Space Brat,* and *I Left My Sneakers in Dimension X.*

Name _____ Date _____

UNDERSTAND THE SITUATION

Directions: Using the skill steps we studied, complete this story.

"Mrs. Jones' fifth grade class was out of the room for recess. When the class returned, Bob discovered that his wallet and money were no longer in his desk. Beth had returned to the room before the class to get her jump rope."

_____

_____

_____

_____

_____

_____

_____

_____

_____

_____

_____

Name _____ Date _____

FAMILY INTERVIEW

Directions:

Interview members of your family to discover what happened when they failed to understand the total situation BEFORE taking action.

_____

_____

_____

_____

_____

_____

_____

SOCIAL SKILL
Avoiding Thoughtless Actions

Behavioral Objective: The students will learn that it is necessary to understand the situation fully before taking action.

Directed Lesson:

1. ***Establish the Need:*** Teacher establishes the need for understanding the entire situation before taking action. It is necessary to think before acting and to determine what occurred to precipitate the situation. Students will learn to attack the problem, rather than the person.

2. ***Introduction:*** Discuss with the class how many times they have been hurt physically or emotionally because either they or someone else acted without thinking. Recognize that thoughtless actions can cause pain even if there is no deliberate intent to do so.

3. ***Identify the Skill Components:***

    1. Be attentive to the situation before taking action.
    2. Talk to a neutral person.
    3. Determine the cause of the situation.
    4. Determine the problem and reason.
    5. Ask for clarification of the situation.

4. ***Model the Skill:*** Teacher displays pictures showing different moods and/or situations, e.g., grief, conflict, exuberance, etc. Students base their reactions on their interpretations of the situation.

5. ***Behavioral Rehearsal:***

    A. ***Selection:*** Teacher selects students for role play.

    B. ***Role Play:*** Divide students into groups; distribute magazine pictures. Let students create scenes with positive reactions then let them solve their problem situations after investigating all angles and having a total picture of the situation.

    C. ***Completion:*** After each role play, reinforce correct behavior, identify inappropriate behaviors, and reenact role play with corrections. If there are no corrections, role play is complete.

    D. ***Reinforcers:*** Awards, verbal praise, repetition of role plays by another group.

    E. ***Discussion:*** Students will discuss the necessity of correctly assessing the situation before reacting.

6. ***Practice:*** Distribute copies of the activity sheet entitled "Scrambled Words" and have students complete it in class. Upon completion, share how the scrambled words are applicable. Answers are: 1. ASK, 2. WATCH, 3. WAIT, 4. QUESTION, 5. LISTEN, 6. THINK, 7. OBSERVE, 8. SITUATION, 9. ACTION.

7. ***Independent Use:*** Give students copies of the following activity sheet entitled "Sentence Sense" to complete at home. They are to decipher the activity sheet using capital letters, spaces, and punctuation as needed. The answers are the skill components. The students will discuss the Social Skill learned at school with an adult at home, then return the activity sheet signed by an adult and relate their home discussions to the class and teacher.

8. ***Continuation:*** Teachers should continue pointing out the need for this skill as related situations arise.

SCRAMBLED WORDS

Directions: The scrambled words below offer clues to this Social Skill. Unscramble the words and write them correctly.

1. k s a   _____

2. c a w t h   _____

3. i t a w   _____

4. t o q u e s i e n   _____

5. n e t i l s   _____

6. k n i t h   _____

7. v o r b e s e   _____

8. o t i a s u n t i   _____

9. t i c o a n   _____

Name _____ Date _____

SENTENCE SENSE

Directions: Use capital letters, proper spacing, and punctuation marks to produce good sentences. Then write the correct sentence on the appropriate line.

1. beattentivetothesituationbeforetakingaction _____

_____

_____

2. determinethecauseofthesituation _____

_____

_____

3. talktoaneutralpersonaboutthesituation _____

_____

_____

4. askforclarificationofthesituation _____

_____

_____

SOCIAL SKILL
Being a Good Listener

Behavioral Objective: The student will listen attentively when the teacher or another class member is speaking to the teacher or class.

Directed Lesson:

1. **Establish the Need:** Stress to the class that listening is our clue to all that goes on around us.

2. **Introduction:** The teacher will read the following story to the class:

   "One day the teacher gave the students permission slips to fill out and take home for their parents to sign for a trip to the museum. Two boys, Terry and Joe, did not pay attention. They did not fill out the slips and take them home to be signed. What do you think happened next?"

   Ask why it is important to listen. (*Sample responses:* to know what to do, and how to do it; to follow directions, etc.). Ask the class what might happen if we don't listen. (*Sample responses:* won't know what to do; might make mistakes; could be harmed.)

3. **Identify the Skill Components:** (List on the board.)

   1. Stop what you are doing.
   2. Sit quietly at your seat.
   3. Look at the speaker.
   4. Ignore distractions.
   5. Think about what you heard.
   6. Ask questions if you need to for understanding.
   7. Repeat the information to yourself.

4. **Model the Skill:** Choose a student to read the following information written on an index card: **"Boys and girls, I'm going to tell you about the lunch procedure. Get your envelope from the back table. Put your money inside. Take it to the lunch aide, then pick up your lunch."** The teacher then teaches the students how to listen to the student that reads the information by using the skill steps on the board.

5. **Behavioral Rehearsal:**

   A. **Selection:** Students volunteer to role play.

   B. **Role Play:** Use the following situations:

1. Student listens as teacher gives a spelling assignment: **"Take out your spelling book. Turn to page 124. Do exercises A, B, skip C and do D."** Student repeats the assignment.

2. Student listens to another student read a short report: **"Ohio is located in the northeastern part of the U.S. Its capital is Columbus. Its boundaries are Lake Erie (N), Pennsylvania (E), West Virginia (SE), Kentucky (S), and Indiana (W)."** Student repeats the information.

C. ***Completion:*** After each role play, reinforce correct behavior, identify inappropriate behaviors, and reenact role play with corrections. If there are no corrections, role play is complete.

D. ***Reinforcers:*** Verbal praise, nonverbal encouragers (smile, pat, etc.), material rewards, chart recognition.

E. ***Discussion:*** Discuss results of role playing.

6. ***Practice:*** Distribute copies of the following activity sheet, "Listen to Learn" and complete it with the class.

7. ***Independent Use:***

A. Students divide into groups and tell each other about their weekend. One student will call on another student to paraphrase what he or she said.

B. A student will ask a parent to read a short news article to him/her. The student will tell the parent what he/she heard. The student will then write down how much or little he heard and bring it to school to share it with the class.

8. ***Continuation:*** Teachers should continue pointing out the need for being a good listener.

CHILDREN'S LITERATURE

Fitzhugh, Louise. *Harriet the Spy.* 1964. Harper Collins.

A good read-aloud chapter book. Have students determine how Harriet puts listening skills to work.

Name _____ Date _____

LISTEN TO LEARN

Climb aboard the Learning Train. Fill in the spaces by writing in the skills for listening, in the correct order.

SKILLS
- Thinking about what's said
- Ask questions
- Make eye contact
- Repeat information
- Stop what you're doing
- Ignore distractions

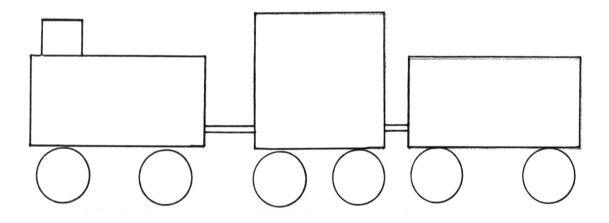

You did it! Good job!

SOCIAL SKILL
Following Verbal Directions

Behavioral Objective: The student will follow verbal directions.

Directed Lesson:

1. ***Establish the Need:*** Review with the students the importance of listening, especially when following directions. Ask what might happen if we didn't listen in order to follow directions.(Sample responses: mistakes made, could cause an accident, etc.)

2. ***Introduction:*** Teacher gives directions for task. How best can class learn to follow verbal directions?

3. ***Identify the Skill Components:*** (List on board.)

    1. Sit quietly and look directly at the speaker.

    2. Ignore unnecessary distractions.

    3. Think about information given.

    4. Ask questions to help understanding.

    5. Carry out the directions.

4. ***Model the Skill:*** Choose a student to read the following directions while you (the teacher) show the steps in carrying out the directions: **"Pick up your pencil and on your paper write your name, date of birth, name one of you parents, and the number of students in the classroom."**

5. ***Behavioral Rehearsal:***

    A. ***Selection:*** Two student volunteers will role play, one giving the directions, and the other one following the directions.

    B. ***Role Play:*** "Line up at milk counter. Go first to the milk bin, next the fruit bin, to the main lunch corner, and last to your seating area."

      Have the class play a game of "Simon Says."

    C. ***Completion:*** After each role play, reinforce correct behavior, identify inappropriate behaviors, and reenact role play with corrections. If there are no corrections, role play is complete.

    D. ***Reinforcers:*** Verbal praise, nonverbal expressions of approval (smile, pat, etc.), group encouragement.

6. ***Practice:*** Distribute copies of the activity sheet entitled "A Lesson Was Learned" for individual completion in the classroom or at home.

7. ***Independent Use:*** Keep a chart in the classroom for playground and lunchroom good listeners. Have students keep a log on how well they follow verbal directions at home.

8. ***Continuation:*** Teachers should continue pointing out the importance of following verbal directions, whenever they are given.

CHILDREN'S LITERATURE

Raskin, Ellen. *The Westing Game.* NY: Dutton, 1978.

In this Newbery award-winning chapter book, the reader (or listener) has to be alert to verbal clues.

Name _____   Date _____

A LESSON WAS LEARNED

Directions: Read the story and answer the following questions:

Joe was a new student in the classroom. He was friendly, but had some bad habits. He liked to talk and play when he was supposed to be listening to the teacher or someone else giving information and directions.

On one occasion, the class was going on a field trip to the zoo. The teacher told everyone that permission slips must be turned in before anyone could go. Also, lunches had to be brought in brown bags, and money could be brought for souvenirs. While the teacher was giving the information about the trip, Joe was playing with his pencil, turning around in his seat, and standing up to see who had dropped a book. When the teacher asked for questions about the trip, Joe didn't say anything.

On the day of the trip, Joe did not bring his permission slip, his lunch money, or any money to spend because he thought the trip was the next day. The teacher asked him how he could have made a mistake like that when she had given all the needed information. Joe lowered his head, and admitted that he had not paid close attention.

Too bad, Joe ended up not having fun going to the zoo with the rest of the class. He had to stay at school and do school work.

* * * * * * * * * * * * * * *

1. What lesson did Joe learn? _____

   _____

2. What was Joe doing when he was supposed to be listening? _____

   _____

3. What steps should Joe have followed while the teacher was giving information? ____

   _____

4. If you don't listen when someone is talking to you, what could happen? _____

   _____

LISTENING

SOCIAL SKILL
Ability to Sit and Listen Quietly

Behavioral Objective: The student will have eye contact with the speaker and sit quietly when someone is talking.

Directed Lesson:

1. **Establish the Need:** By listening carefully, the student will better understand verbal directions and the material presented, and will show politeness to the speaker. As a result, he/she should experience more success in school activities.

2. **Introduction:** The teacher will read the following story.

> **"One day in Mr. Spencer's gym class, he told the students that they were going to learn how to play a new game. He told them that they must sit quietly and pay attention to the instructions, because there was not enough time during the period to repeat them for each person. If they did not listen to learn the rules, they would be excluded. While Mr. Spencer was giving the instructions and showing the class how to play the game, two boys, Terry and Joe, were hitting each other and talking to each other. When it was time to play the game, the two boys did not know how to play. They asked Mr. Spencer to repeat the instructions, but since they had not listened, they were told to sit and watch the others play. They were very angry, but they were excluded from the game."**

(1) Why were they excluded? (2) Whose fault was it? (3) Was this fair? (4) What should they have done?

3. **Identify the Skill Components:** (List on board before class.)

   A good listener will:

   a. Keep eyes on who is talking.

   b. Sit quietly when someone is talking.

   c. Listen to the person who is talking.

4. **Model the Skill:**

   A. The teacher will select a short one or two paragraph story and have it read to the class by a student. The students will tell the story to the teacher in sequence. The teacher will model the behavior by looking at the reader and sitting quietly when the story is read.

31

    B. The class will watch part of an art program on television. After the partial program, they will gather needed materials and complete the art project. Students should take notes during the broadcast to help them remember the materials and steps needed to complete the art project.

5. Behavioral Rehearsal:

    A. ***Selection:*** Teacher selects groups of students to role play.

    B. ***Role Play:*** Students in each group role play situations in which one student reads a story or gives instructions and the other students follow the skill steps. Some of the students will be asked to retell the story as they heard it. Repeat with different students.

    C. ***Completion:*** After each role play, reinforce correct behavior, identify inappropriate behaviors, and reenact role play with corrections. If there are no corrections, role play is complete.

    D. ***Reinforcers:*** Teacher should encourage correct behaviors with verbal praise.

    E. ***Discussion:*** Discuss the students' observations of the roles and why the skill is necessary.

6. ***Practice:*** Distribute copies of the activity sheet entitled "Find a Good Listener" and play the game together in class.

7. ***Independent Use:*** Give students copies of the following "Good Listener Chart." Have all members of the class keep the chart for two days, then give a prize to the winner.

8. ***Continuation:*** Teachers should continue to remind students of the need for this skill as related situations arise, using catchy phrases such as **"Good manners never go out of style."**

© 1996 by SPV

Name _____   Date _____

FIND A GOOD LISTENER

1. Social Skill: LISTENING

2. Skill Steps:
A GOOD LISTENER WILL
   a. Keep eyes on the speaker
   b. Sit quietly while someone is talking

3. Activity Title: "FIND A GOOD LISTENER"

A. Directions: This activity is to be done with the whole class. Review the skill steps for a good listener. At the end of the school day, students will vote by secret ballot for a student who consistently followed the skill steps for good listening.

B. Some Rules To Remember Are:
   1. Don't vote for yourself.
   2. Vote for someone who followed good listening rules.
   3. The student who gets the most votes will receive a treat.

WHO GETS YOUR VOTE? _____

(This activity can be done whenever the need arises to reinforce the social skill).

Name _____ Date _____

GOOD LISTENER CHART

1. Social Skill—Listening:

2. Skill Steps:

   A good listener will:

   a. Keep eyes on the speaker.

   b. Sit quietly when someone is talking.

3. Activity directions:

   Each student will choose several students and check if they are using good listening skills.

Name	Eye Contact					Sits Quietly				
1. _____										
2. _____										
3. _____										
4. _____										
5. _____										

Which student was the best listener? _____

LISTENING Lesson 10

SOCIAL SKILL
Paraphrasing What Is Heard

Behavioral Objective: The student will be attentive to what is said and will be able to explain it in his/her own words afterwards.

Directed Lesson:

1. **Establish the Need:** The importance of the skill lies in the basic assumption that listening is required for participation in the majority of life's activities. When we think of being deaf for even a minute or an hour, we can readily appreciate how important the sense of hearing is. To learn to retell what you hear is equally important for the purpose of communication with others.

   The discussion will begin with the definition of the term *listening,* which can be looked up in the dictionary. After analyzing its meaning, the teacher will write a synthesizing sentence on the board which is appropriate for the grade level being taught.

2. **Introduction:** The following story will be read by the teacher.

   "Kenita was busily working on her reading skills assignment. She was making an outline of a paragraph from her social studies book. All of a sudden there was a loud thump. A student named Terrell had fainted after receiving his science test. Needless to say, the class was disrupted and the student had to be taken to the hospital for X-rays. Whether Terrell did well or poorly on the test was a mystery to Kenita. She had other things to worry about, namely her outline."

   Discussion:

   1. A student is asked to paraphrase the story and to include the original basic details of the story.
   2. The class then evaluates the student's response as compared to the original. If there is a need for clarification, the teacher will read the story again.

3. **Identify the Skill Components:** (List on board before class.)

   1. Sit in an upright position free from distractions such as pencils and papers and listen attentively.
   2. Focus attention on the presentation being given.
   3. Make a mental outline of what is said for possible retelling or paraphrasing later.

4. **Model the Skill:** Following the skill steps, the teacher will ask a student to read a short story or poem and paraphrase the story correctly.

5. ***Behavioral Rehearsal:***

   A. ***Selection:*** Teacher selects four pairs of students to role play.

   B. ***Role Play:***

     1. Students at these grade levels should be able to take four numbers such as 25, 61, 43, and 78, and tell immediately what the sum of the four numbers is equal to. Select about five students to do this activity. The numbers should be given only once verbally. Calculations are to be done mentally, and not on paper.

     2. The teacher or students will read a short poem. The students should be able to recite this poem exactly from memory.

     3. The teacher or students will read short articles from the newspaper. The students should be able to paraphrase the article from memory.

   C. ***Completion:*** After each role play, reinforce correct behavior, identify inappropriate behaviors, and reenact role play with corrections. If there are no corrections, role play is complete.

   D. ***Reinforcers:*** After each role play, teacher asks each student to name something they learned during the role play. Teacher provides verbal praise.

   E. ***Discussion:*** Discuss the necessity for good listening and the problems that may occur when it is not employed.

     1. Lack of knowledge.

     2. Danger to an individual: not being attentive

     3. Poor academic work.

     4. Inability to participate fully in some activity.

6. ***Practice:*** Distribute copies of the following two activity sheets to the class. The first, entitled "Listening Survey," asks each student to rate how well he/she listens in various situations. This one should be completed first. The second, entitled "My Best Listening," asks the student to describe his/her best listening habit or activity.

7. ***Independent Use:*** Students will watch a television show at home and will paraphrase the plot to the class. The class will evaluate the report and give suggestions for improvement.

8. ***Continuation:*** Teacher tells the students that being able to listen well is one key to success in school and in the future. Periodically, ask students to tell what they learned that day in school that required listening.

CHILDREN'S LITERATURE

Set up a Media Corner and have students listen to books on tape that can be secured from the public library.

Name _____ Date _____

LISTENING SURVEY

Directions: In order to see how well (or how poorly) you listen, complete the following survey. You will rate yourself on each statement as to how well or how poorly you listen using a number scale from 1 to 5.

Scale

1 means "I don't listen at all."

2 means "I listen once in awhile."

3 means "I sometimes listen."

4 means "I listen most of the time."

5 means "I listen all of the time."

Circle the number for each sentence that you feel best describes how you listen in the situation described.

1. I listen to my parents.	1	2	3	4	5
2. I listen to my teacher in class.	1	2	3	4	5
3. I listen to my teacher outside of class.	1	2	3	4	5
4. I listen to the gym teacher.	1	2	3	4	5
5. I listen to people older than myself.	1	2	3	4	5
6. I listen to people younger than myself.	1	2	3	4	5
7. I listen to the radio or other music.	1	2	3	4	5
8. I listen at assemblies or gatherings.	1	2	3	4	5
9. I listen to the lunchroom workers.	1	2	3	4	5
10. I listen to the school guards.	1	2	3	4	5
11. I listen to my brothers and/or sisters.	1	2	3	4	5
12. I listen for sounds of danger.	1	2	3	4	5

How do you rate as a listener?

Name _____ Date _____

MY BEST LISTENING

Directions: Now that you have had a chance to think about your listening habits, select ONE of the 12 numbers where you circled the number Scale 5 meaning that you listened all the time. Write a paragraph explaining why.

_____

_____

_____

_____

_____

_____

_____

MAKE A PICTURE TO ACCOMPANY THE PARAGRAPH.

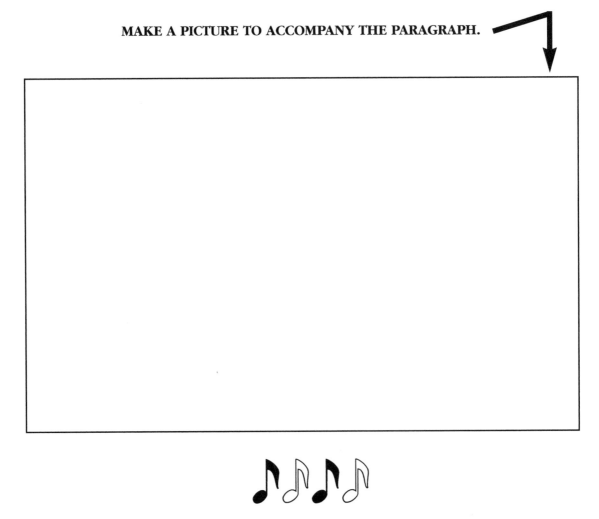

SOCIAL SKILL

Ability to Listen/Participate in Class Discussion

Behavioral Objective: The student will exhibit attentive behavior during instruction and class discussion.

Directed Lesson:

1. **Establish the Need:** Listening is a skill that is basic to learning. This skill should be learned early as it is needed for any class discussions and for following instructions.

2. **Introduction:** Read the following story:

   "Mr. Green's class at (your school) was told that they would be seeing a movie and that following it, they would have to answer questions. Mr. Green reminded the class to pay close attention to the movie. The class enjoyed the show and insisted that they had paid close attention to it. When the activity sheets were distributed, the class was instructed to complete them. After checking the responses, Mr. Green found that some students were unable to answer the questions correctly."

   The teacher asks the class: **"Why do you think that some of the students were unable to complete the worksheet correctly?"**

3. **Identify the Skill Components:** (List on board before class.)

   1. Prepare yourself to listen (clean up, stop talking).
   2. Look at the person speaking.
   3. Think about what is being presented.
   4. Respond by nodding, asking or answering questions, repeating.

4. **Model the Skill:** Ask the class to suggest someone they feel is a good listener to serve as a model in the demonstration. Ask that child if he/she wants to participate. If not, ask the class to raise hands and offer another suggestion. After a model is chosen, divide the rest of the clan into 4 groups. Appoint each group to watch for and later report on how well all the skill steps have been modeled (one group per skill step). Encourage student to think aloud. "I think I'll sit next to Bobby because we usually do not disturb each other during presentations or instructions."

5. **Behavioral Rehearsal:**

   A. **Selection:** Ask students to form small groups of five.

B. ***Role Play:*** Have one student in each group assume the role of discussion leader. Have two students to take turns telling each other something that is important to them, while the others listen attentively. The leader will then ask the listeners to review/recall what each student said. The rest of the class will watch for behaviors in the process of good listening. Each group role plays in front of the class.

C. ***Completion:*** After each role play, reinforce correct behavior, identify inappropriate behaviors, and reenact role play with corrections. If there are no corrections, role play is complete.

D. ***Reinforcers:*** Verbal praise from teacher and peers.

E. ***Discussion:*** Critique not only how the listeners focused their attention, but also how they responded to the speaker (nodded, smiled, asked an appropriate question, etc.).

6. ***Practice:*** Distribute copies of the following activity sheet entitled "Listening." The teacher will read the following instructions only once. They will *not* be repeated:

A. Write your *Name* on Line 3.

B. Write the word *Red* on Line 5.

C. Write your *Classroom Number* on Line 1.

D. Write the *Day* on Line 2.

E. Write your *Favorite Food* on Line 4.

7. ***Independent Use:*** Students should listen to the weather report on television and report to the class when asked. The teacher must also watch the report to check the accuracy of the answers. The teacher will request listening to a specific station.

8. ***Continuation:*** Teachers should remind students of the importance of being able to follow instructions in all areas of our lives.

CHILDREN'S LITERATURE

Fritz, Jean. *What's the Big Idea, Ben Franklin?* Illustrated by Margaret Tomes. NY: Coward, 1982.

A good read-aloud book filled with a great deal of factual information. What can students learn about this man by *listening* to a fascinating story?

Name _____ Date _____

LISTENING

Follow directions given by the teacher.

1. _____

2. _____

3. _____

4. _____

5. _____

How well did you listen?

SOCIAL SKILL
Attending to the Speaker

Behavioral Objective: The student will listen attentively when the teacher or another student is talking to the class.

Directed Lesson:

1. ***Establish the Need:*** Review with the students how important good listening skills are to improve academic success.

2. ***Introduction:*** Ask the students to do a short assignment and you will give the directions. Tell them to listen very carefully so that they will not miss any information. After checking the responses from the papers, ask why some students were able to answer the questions correctly and some were not.

3. ***Identify the Skill Components:*** (List on board before class.)

   1. Look at the person speaking.
   2. Do not make funny facial expressions or move around (sit quietly).
   3. Always concentrate on what is being said.
   4. If asked a question, indicate that you have heard it by answering or nodding your head. You might need to raise your hand.
   5. Ask questions if you do not understand.

4. ***Model the Skill:*** Teacher models the skill by having a student read the directions to a game and then following the directions. Show the students how to follow the skill steps. Stress the importance of listening carefully to everything said.

5. ***Behavioral Rehearsal:***

   A. ***Selection:*** Select three students to role play in sequence.

   B. ***Role Play:*** Ask the three students to give directions to the class. Check the responses to see how well the class did in listening to the directions.

   C. ***Completion:*** After each role play, reinforce correct behavior, identify inappropriate behaviors, and reenact role play with corrections. If there are no corrections, role play is complete.

   D. ***Reinforcers:*** Good listening badges, verbal praise, group reinforcement, improved grades.

   E. ***Discussion:*** Discuss how well the role plays were accomplished and how good the presenter was in giving directions and responses. Discuss what the students who did not listen well could do to correct their behaviors.

6. ***Practice:*** Play a cassette tape of a story to the class. After the cassette has ended, ask the students to answer questions based on the taped story. Then relisten to the tape and correct the answers. Also complete the following activity sheet "How Good Are You at Following Directions," that is included in this lesson.

7. ***Independent Use:*** Ask colleagues in the school, such as the librarian, physical education teacher, and lunch aides to emphasize giving directions once and watching the response for the next two weeks. Report their observations to the teacher.

   Distribute the second activity sheet "Who's a Good Listener?" and ask the students to take it home and draw a picture of a friend or family member who is a good listener, and write a story about him/her. At a date given by the teacher, the students will return the completed activity sheet for discussion in class.

8. ***Continuation:*** Teacher tells students that the more carefully they listen to others, the better others will listen to them.

CHILDREN'S LITERATURE

Hamilton, Virginia. *The People Could Fly.* Alfred A. Knopf, 1985.

This collection of African folktales is a good read-aloud choice. It is also available on audiotape, and provides good opportunities for repeated listening to the tales.

Name _____ Date _____

HOW GOOD ARE YOU AT FOLLOWING DIRECTIONS?

Directions: This activity may be conducted verbally or it may be a written exercise.

1. Write your name on a piece of notebook paper that has been placed on your desk.

2. Fold this piece of paper in half *vertically*.

3. Number each line starting with number 1 and continue numbering until you reach number 10.

4. Write the names of three colors on lines 1, 2, and 3.

5. Write the name of your school on line 4.

6. Write your teacher's name on line 5.

7. What skill are we working on? Write it on the next line.

8. Draw a smiling face that fills lines 7, 8, 9, and 10.

How well did you do?

WHO'S A GOOD LISTENER?

Draw this person's picture in the space.

_____ *is, because*

Name

_____

_____

_____

FOLLOWING INSTRUCTIONS

SOCIAL SKILL

Following Specific Instructions

Behavior Objective: The student will follow higher-level instructions which involve various steps.

Directed Lesson:

1. **Establish the Need:** The importance of the skill lies in the fact that many activities involve the completion of specific directions or instructions. Not following instructions can lead to failure, frustration, and anger.

2. **Introduction:** The discussion will begin with the importance of careful listening so that instructions may be followed precisely. The word instruction should be defined.

   The following story will be read which illustrates the importance of following instructions whether verbal or written.

   "Ramus went to Pick-N-Pay to buy many kinds of food. He went through the whole store and stopped at the bakery last. The cream puffs in the window captured his eye as well as the lemon chiffon pie. Because he was so busy dreaming about the delicious goodies, he failed to notice the sign which said, 'Please take a number and wait patiently.' Ramus began to notice that people had numbers in their hands and they were being waited on. Finally, he asked someone and they told him to read the sign. Five people had been waited on ahead of him because of his lack of attention, and someone had purchased those beautiful cream puffs he was served."

   The following questions will be discussed:

   1. What mistake did Ramus make at first?
   2. What were the consequences of Ramus's not following instructions?
   3. What other more important situation can you think of where following instructions could be quite important?

3. **Identify the Skill Components:** (List on board before class.)

   1. The person needs to be attentive and alert to the instructions around him/her.
   2. If a verbal instruction is being given, the person must be conscious of the instruction and be applying it to the situation at the time.
   3. If the instruction is unclear, it should be clarified or questioned.

4. **Model the Skill:** The teacher will follow a set of directions read by the student to illustrate the skill.

46

5. ***Behavioral Rehearsal:***

   A. ***Selection:*** Teacher selects a pair of students to role play each activity. Then large group role play can be used.

   B. ***Role play:***

      1. The teacher will instruct the students in making a game such as tic-tac-toe. This can be made using construction paper and/or wallpaper pieces on a cardboard backing.

      2. If a waffle or pizzelle maker is available, the class can make these. The teacher assigns the responsibilities to groups and the instructions are followed in the order of the groups.

      3. During wintertime making snowflakes is a good activity for following instructions since failure to complete even one step can result in a mistake.

   C. ***Completion:*** After each role play, reinforce correct behavior, identify inappropriate behaviors, and reenact role play with corrections. If there are no corrections, role play is complete.

   D. ***Reinforcers:*** Materials produced, verbal praise, peer praise.

   E. ***Discussion:*** Students will discuss role plays and group activities and positive and negative aspects of each.

6. ***Practice:*** Distribute copy of the following activity sheet entitled "Where Are You Now?" and read to the students the activity sheet "Verbal Instructions for Following Map."

7. ***Independent Use:*** Have students bring a signed note by parents showing they followed verbal directions to complete an assignment using instructions at home.

8. ***Continuation:*** Teacher tells students that using this skill each and every day will help them feel good inside and to do well in school.

CHILDREN'S LITERATURE

Kerr, M. E. *Love Is a Missing Person.* Laurel Leaf, 1975.

Name _____ Date _____

WHERE ARE YOU NOW?

Directions: The teacher will read a set of instructions which you will follow on the map below. They will be read only once, so listen carefully. For this, you will need a pencil.

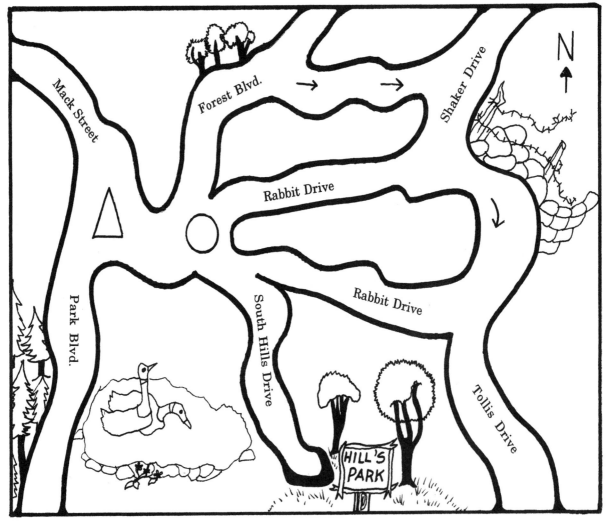

In a sentence, tell whether or not this was a challenging activity.

_____

_____

_____

_____

VERBAL INSTRUCTIONS FOR FOLLOWING MAP

1. You are now at the top left of the map where Mack Street starts.

2. Now go south and stop at the triangular intersection of Park Boulevard and Mack Street.

3. Go east to Rabbit Drive and make a full circular turn on Rabbit Drive and come around to the intersection marked with the circle.

4. Next, go north on Forest Boulevard and take the one-way shortcut to Shaker Drive.

5. Go south on Shaker Drive to Rabbit Drive and make a full circular turn and come around to the intersection marked with the circle.

6. Make a left turn by going south on South Hills Drive until it ends.

7. Where are you now? Make an "X" there and put your pencil away.

ANSWER: The park on South Hills Drive.

VARIATIONS: Make up your own unique instructions for students to follow.

FOLLOWING INSTRUCTIONS

Lesson 14

SOCIAL SKILL
Ability to Follow Verbal Directions

Behavioral Objective: The student will learn to listen and follow verbal directions.

Directed Lesson:

1. ***Establish the Need:*** Discuss the importance of following directions. What happens if you don't follow instructions?

2. ***Introduction:*** Have a spelling bee with specific instructions and eliminate those students who don't follow the directions. Using graph paper, give map location directions to the class. Those students who do not listen will have a different map at the end of the assignment. Be sure to inject humor into the lesson so students do not feel stressed about not following instructions. Discuss the results of doing the work after carefully following directions and the results of not following them carefully enough.

3. ***Identify the Skill Components:*** (List on board before class.)

   1. Look at the speaker.
   2. Think about what is being said.
   3. Ask for more information if needed.
   4. Take notes.
   5. Follow instructions.
   6. If you succeed, praise yourself.

4. ***Model the Skill:*** The teacher will ask a student to read instructions that he/she will listen to and follow them. Be sure that the teacher role plays the steps on the board.

5. ***Behavioral Rehearsal:***

   A. ***Selection:*** Teacher selects students to role play giving instructions to the class. Quantity will depend on number of instructions.

   B. ***Role Play:*** Have instructions written on file cards for the students to read to the class. Ask students to answer on paper. Walk around and observe the responses on the papers.

   C. ***Completion:*** After each role play, reinforce correct behavior, identify inappropriate behaviors, and reenact role play with corrections. If there are no corrections, role play is complete.

   D. ***Reinforcers:*** These include word puzzles, award badges for good listening, progress cards, verbal praise, and improved grades.

50

E. ***Discussion:*** Discuss the answers from the role plays and re-emphasize the correct listening steps. Compare the results of correct and incorrect papers.

6. ***Practice:*** Ask the class to take out a piece of paper to use for this assignment. Explain that you will read all six directions before they are to begin working. Stress that the students should listen carefully and make no comments about the directions. Then, repeat the instructions and allow the students enough time to complete each instruction.

DIRECTIONS TO READ: Listen carefully to all the instructions before you start this assignment.

1. Divide a sheet of paper into four sections by folding the paper twice.
2. Draw a house in the upper left section of the paper.
3. Draw a car with four wheels and one large window in the lower left section of the paper.
4. Write Roman numerals from 1 to 50 in the upper right corner of the paper.
5. Draw a square, rectangle, triangle and circle in the lower right corner.

7. ***Independent Use:*** Students will keep individual tallies that indicate the amount of times they have followed instructions correctly in school and at home.

8. ***Continuation:*** Teachers tell students, **"If you use this skill whenever and wherever you need it, you will prevent many problems and learn more quickly in school."**

SOCIAL SKILL
Feeling Good About Oneself

Behavioral Objective: The students will tell three things they can do well, and explain why they feel they are good at doing them.

Directed Lesson:

1. **Establish the Need:** Discuss the importance of feeling good about oneself. *Sample responses:* It makes a person feel valued; it makes one feel needed by others, etc. Ask how persons might feel if they don't feel good about themselves. *Sample responses:* Hard to get along with; might do harm to others, etc.

2. **Identify the Skill Components:** (List on board.)

    1. Think about things you can do well.

    2. Choose three things.

    3. Tell what they are, and give reasons why you feel you can do them well.

3. **Model the Skill:** Select a volunteer student to ask you (the teacher) to describe three things you can do well. The teacher then demonstrates how one goes about expressing these three things in sentences.

4. **Behavioral Rehearsal:**

    A. **Selection:** Have students volunteer to role play.

    B. **Role Play:** Ask students to name three things they can do well, and explain in complete sentences why they think they do them well.

    C. **Completion:** After each role play, reinforce correct behavior, identify inappropriate behaviors, and reenact role play with corrections. If there are no corrections, role play is complete.

    D. **Reinforcers:** Verbal praise, nonverbal approval, group reinforcement.

    E. **Discussion:** Discuss results of role plays.

5. **Practice:** Distribute copies of the activity sheet entitled "Toot Your Own Horn!" and have students complete it in class.

6. **Independent Usage:** Give students copies of the activity sheet entitled "Things We Do Well." Students are to go around the room asking classmates whether they can do things on the list, and have them sign their names next to the item.

7. **Continuation:** Teacher reminds students, **"If you think good thoughts about yourself, you will make more friends and find it easier to learn new things."**

Name _____ Date _____

TOOT YOUR OWN HORN !

Write or draw three things you can do well at home, school, or play. Be able to tell why.

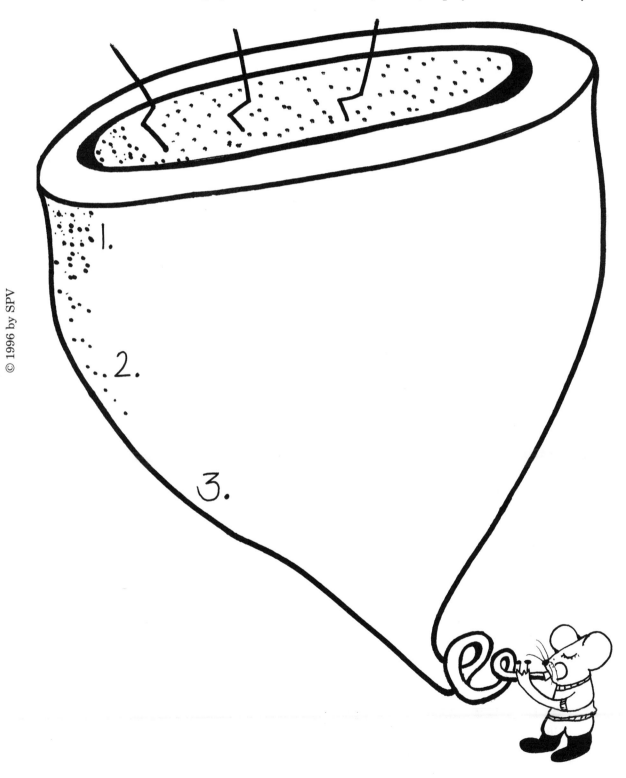

Name _____ Date _____

THINGS WE DO WELL

Directions: Find someone in your class who can do one of the following. Try to get as many different names as possible. Have each person sign his/her name.

1. A person who has bowled and got a strike _____

2. A person who has received an A on a paper _____

3. A person who has received recognition for being helpful _____

4. Someone who has won a contest _____

5. Someone who ran in a race and finished _____

6. A person who read ten books over the summer _____

7. Someone who keeps his/her desk clean and neat _____

8. A person who can sing or dance _____

9. A person who can play an instrument _____

10. Someone who is responsible for a younger brother or sister _____

11. A person who can ice skate or roller skate _____

12. A person who is good in art _____

13. Someone who is a member of the Scouts _____

14. Someone who can do housework (dishes, cleaning, etc.) _____

15. A person who has received an A for citizenship _____

16. A person who has caught a fly ball or made a home run _____

17. Someone who can set up and work AV equipment _____

18. A person who has planted a garden _____

19. Someone who comes to school every day _____

20. A person who plays on a Little League team _____

SOCIAL SKILL

Helping Another Person

Behavioral Objective: The student will tell something he/she has done to help another person.

Directed Lesson:

1. **Establish the Need:** Ask the students how they feel when they have helped someone. (*Sample responses:* good, proud, pleased, happy, etc.) Ask why we need to help each other. What might happen if we didn't help each other?

2. **Identify the Skill Components:** (List on board.)

    1. Think about how you have helped others.

    2. Select one situation to express what you did.

    3. Tell what you did in complete sentences.

3. **Model the Skill:** Teacher tells about how he/she has helped others using the above components.

4. **Behavioral Rehearsal:**

    A. **Selection:** Have students volunteer to role play the following:

    B. **Role Play:**

       1. **Situation:** Student walks and drops books. The other student comes along and helps student pick up books.

       2. **Situation:** Student doing a hard math problem looks puzzled. Another student comes to his aid and helps solve problem.

    C. **Completion:** After each role play, reinforce correct behavior, identify inappropriate behaviors, and reenact role play with corrections. If there are no corrections, role play is complete.

    D. **Reinforcers:** Material rewards, verbal praise, nonverbal approval, class chart entitled "Helper of the Day."

    E. **Discussion:** Have another student ask the helping students in the role plays how they helped someone today and how they felt about it.

5. **Practice:** Distribute copies of the activity sheet entitled "Blue Ribbon" for students to complete and share in class.

6. **Independent Use:** Have students work on a project, such as providing goodies for a nursing home and delivering them, or running a canned food drive for a homeless center.

7. ***Continuation:*** Teacher reminds students how good they will feel about themselves when they have helped someone.

CHILDREN'S LITERATURE

Fleishman, Paul. *The Whipping Boy.* NY: Greenwillow. 1986

An adventure story that contrasts the character of two boys, and shows who is really a prince.

Name _____ Date _____

BLUE RIBBON

HELPFUL PERSON

Tell how you have given help to someone, and how you felt AFTER having given this aid.

_____

_____

_____

_____

_____

_____

_____

_____

_____

Draw a picture in the space above to go with your story.

SOCIAL SKILL
Knowing Yourself

Behavioral Objective: The student will improve his/her self-image by analyzing his/her strengths and weaknesses.

Directed Lesson:

1. **Establish the Need:** You need to feel good about yourself to enhance your academic and social growth.

2. **Introduction:** Teacher tells this story:

   "One day the teacher said, 'We are going to decorate the room for a party. Everyone will help. Write down what job you think you do best, then we will assign jobs to those who can do each best. That way you will do the job you feel best about and will do a good job." After all the jobs were assigned the class did good work."

   How would the students have done if they had been assigned jobs they didn't like?

3. **Identify the Skill Components:** (List on board before class.)

   1. Think about your strengths.
   2. Think about you weaknesses.
   3. Select one thing you do well.
   4. Select one weakness.
   5. Tell one strength.
   6. Tell one weakness, and a solution for conquering the weakness.

4. **Model the Skill:**

   A. Teacher reads this statement to the class: **"The one thing that I really do well is . . . ." "The one thing I think needs improvement is . . . ." "I'll try to improve it by . . . ."**

   B. Have three students model things that they do well and things that need improving.

5. **Behavioral Rehearsal:**

   A. **Selection:** Teacher selects each student to role play the skill.

   B. **Role Play:** Using the statement that the teacher read from above, each student will tell one thing that is his or her strength, and one thing that is his or her weakness and how he/she can conquer the weakness.

C. ***Completion:*** After each role play, reinforce correct behavior, identify inappropriate behaviors, and reenact role play with corrections. If there are no corrections, role play is complete.

D. ***Reinforcers:*** Self-praise, group reinforcement, praise in home environment, material rewards.

E. ***Discussion:*** Discuss benefits of knowing your strong and weak areas in school subjects and in personal habits.

6. ***Practice:*** Distribute copies of the activity sheet entitled "Knowing Myself" and have students complete it together in class.

7. ***Independent Use:*** Give students copies of the activity sheet entitled "Things I Do Well" to complete at home. They are to have a friend and a family member list one thing they feel the student does well, then sign the sheet. The activity sheet should be returned within one week.

8. ***Continuation:*** Teachers will remind students that each of us has special strengths as well as weaknesses and that we can improve our weaknesses if we try.

CHILDREN'S LITERATURE

Dakos, Kalli. *If You're Not Here, Please Raise Your Hand.* Illustrated by G. Brian Karas. A poetry book about school.

Name _____ Date _____

KNOWING MYSELF

Skill Steps:
1. Think about your strengths.
2. Think about your weaknesses.
3. Select one thing you do well.
4. Select one weakness.
5. Describe your strengths.
6. Describe one of your weaknessess and a solution to conquer the weakness.

FILL IN THE BALLONS FOR EACH CATEGORY AND DRAW IN ANY DETAILS TO HIGHLIGHT THE CARTOON.

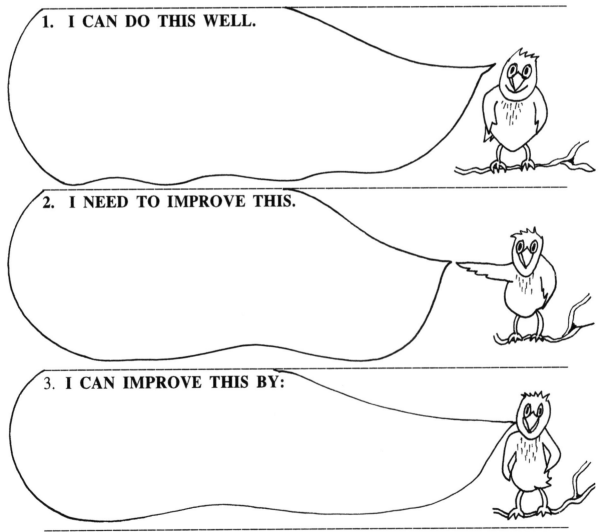

1. I CAN DO THIS WELL.

2. I NEED TO IMPROVE THIS.

3. I CAN IMPROVE THIS BY:

Name _____ Date _____

THINGS I DO WELL

THINGS I DO WELL (as told by a family member and a friend)

* *

1. _____ **does the following well:**

                  (Name)

_____

_____

_____

                                 _____

                                 (Signature of family member)

* *

2. _____ **does the following well:**

                  (Name)

_____

_____

_____

                                 _____

                                 (Signature of friend)

* *

Return the sheet by this date: _____

Lesson 18

SOCIAL SKILL
Recognizing Your Strengths and Weaknesses

Behavioral Objective: The student will improve his/her self-image by analyzing his/her strengths and weaknesses.

Directed Lesson:

1. ***Establish the Need:*** You need to feel good about yourself to enhance your academic and social growth.

2. ***Introduction:*** Teacher will introduce Albert Einstein, famous scientist and creator of the theory of relativity, and Stevie Wonder, famous musician.

    1. Albert Einstein had difficulty with languages and even failed entrance examinations for college the first time he took them.

    2. Stevie Wonder, who has been blind since birth, is one of the most popular musicians since the 1960s.

    3. Discuss the strengths and weaknesses of each.

3. ***Identify the Skill Components:*** (List on board before class.)

    1. Think about your strengths.

    2. Think about your weaknesses.

    3. Select one thing you do well.

    4. Select one weakness.

    5. Describe one strength.

    6. Describe one weakness, and a solution for conquering the weakness.

4. ***Model the Skill:*** Teacher will model the skill by selecting and telling a strength and a weakness, and telling how he/she is improving the weakness.

5. ***Behavioral Rehearsal:***

    A. ***Selection:*** Teacher will select students for each role play.

    B. ***Role Play:*** Each student will select a well-known person to read about. Then they will tell about the person's strengths and weaknesses.

    C. ***Completion:*** After each role play, reinforce correct behavior, identify inappropriate behaviors, and reenact role play with corrections. If there are no corrections, role play is complete.

    D. ***Reinforcers:*** Self-praise, group reinforcement, praise in home environment, material rewards.

    E. ***Discussion:*** Students will discuss how they decided on each strength and weakness and will list the steps used most in the role plays.

6. ***Practice:*** Distribute copies of the activity sheet entitled "Two Great Men" about Albert Einstein and Stevie Wonder, which the students will write a positive statement and also how these two men overcame their individual weaknesses.

7. ***Independent Use:*** Give students copies of the activity sheet entitled "Things I Need to Improve" to complete at home. The students are to have a friend and parent to list some of their weaknesses that need improvement. The activity sheet is to be signed by the friend and the parent and returned within one week.

8. ***Continuation:*** Teachers should continue pointing out the importance of recognizing our own strengths and weaknesses and working to overcome the latter.

CHILDREN'S LITERATURE

There are many fine biographies available about famous people with a variety of talents (sports, music, medicine, the arts, etc.). Have them available from the library for silent reading time.

Name _____ Date _____

TWO GREAT MEN

ALBERT EINSTEIN (SCIENTIST)

_____

_____

_____

_____

_____

_____

_____

* *

STEVIE WONDER (MUSICIAN)

_____

_____

_____

_____

_____

_____

_____

Where can you find information about each person?

Name _____   Date _____

THINGS I NEED TO IMPROVE

1. _____ **needs to improve the following:**

   (Name)

   _____

   _____

   _____

                                    _____

                                    (Signature of parent)

* *

2. _____ **needs to improve the following:**

   (Name)

   _____

   _____

   _____

                                    _____

                                    (Signature of friend)

Return the sheet by this date: _____

SOCIAL SKILL
Understanding Our Uniqueness

Behavioral Objective: The student will be able to state some quality that makes him/her special.

Directed Lesson:

1. **Establish the Need:** Each person has many qualities unique to him- or herself. It is important for each person to realize these qualities in order to increase feelings of self-worth.

2. **Introduction:** Read this story to the class:

   "In a city much like St. Louis, in a school much like ours, there lived a boy named Lee, who had many friends. He loved and admired his friends because he thought each was so very special. His friend Tom could run as fast as lightning, and his friend Bill was so honest the lunchroom teachers always trusted him with the milk money. His friend Bob was an expert in math, his friend Joe was good at (ask for ideas). Lee felt that every one of his friends was talented, but he didn't think he himself had any special abilities. Now it happened that Lee was absent for six weeks due to a case of pneumonia. When he came back to school, all the students had made cards to greet him back. The cards said, 'Welcome back to the nicest friend anyone could have.' His teacher said, 'Lee always finds the best in everyone! That is a rare and wonderful quality!'"

   Teacher asks the class: **"How do you think Lee felt after receiving the cards? Do you think he felt better about himself?"**

3. **Identify the Skill Components:** (List on board before class.)

   1. Think of many different ways to be special.
   2. Think hard about yourself.
   3. Decide on some special quality you really like about yourself.
   4. State the quality when asked.

4. **Model the Skill:** The teacher and class brainstorm as many ways to be special as they can possibly name and the teacher writes these on the board. Then the teacher models the process of thinking about yourself, circling some of the qualities on the board that might apply to him/her. The teacher selects one quality he/she is most proud of.

5. **Behavioral Rehearsal:**

   A. **Selection:** All students will role play.

B. ***Role Play:*** Have each student choose five qualities from the board that apply to him/her and then choose the one attribute that is most important. Ask volunteers to tell their most important quality. All students must get a turn.

C. ***Completion:*** After each role play, reinforce correct behavior, identify inappropriate behaviors, and reenact role play with corrections. If there are no corrections, role play is complete.

D. ***Reinforcers:*** Badges, peer verbal praise, teacher verbal praise.

E. ***Discussion:*** Students discuss how each person is different and how each person has some unique quality. Ask the students to relate how it felt to tell everyone something special about themselves.

6. ***Practice:*** Each day, choose one student's name from a hat. Ask that student to leave the room. Lead the class as they brainstorm all the positive attributes they can name about that individual. Write the list on construction paper as the students say each quality. The paper may be headed, "YOU ARE SPECIAL!" The list is displayed all day and then taken home by the special student at the end of the day.

7. ***Independent Use:*** Students will write some special quality they have that does not apply to school work and will present this quality to the class when asked. Also, have student ask a family member to listen to the student speaking about a good trait they have.

8. ***Continuation:*** Teachers should continue pointing out the importance of understanding our own special quality.

SOCIAL SKILL

Recognizing One's Special Quality

Behavioral Objective: The student will identify something he/she likes about him- or herself.

Directed Lesson:

1. **Establish the Need:** Review and discuss that building a positive self-image will help individuals academically and socially.

2. **Introduction:** Read a story where the main character does not like something about him- or herself. Follow this with a discussion of why and how it is resolved and how he/she is accepted by others.

3. **Identify the Skill Components:** (List on board before class.)

    1. Think about what you like best about yourself.
    2. Decide why you made that choice.
    3. Decide the best way to share this information.
    4. Think of ways to change things about yourself you don't like.
    5. Ask others to help you change things you don't like about yourself.

4. **Model the Skill:** The teacher will model the skill by saying one thing that he/she likes about himself/herself. Then the teacher tells the class what it is and why it was selected.

5. **Behavioral Rehearsal:**

    A. **Selection:** Include all students.

    B. **Role Play:** Students will decide on a quality that is positive about themselves. Each student will tell their neighbor that quality. Ask students to report any difficulties.

    C. **Completion:** After each role play, reinforce correct behavior, identify inappropriate behaviors, and reenact role play with corrections. If there are no corrections, role play is complete.

    D. **Reinforcers:** Verbal praise, approval, group enforcement, slap on the back.

    E. **Discussion:** Discuss why it is necessary to like yourself, and how you can decide what you like about yourself.

6. **Practice:** Distribute copies of the activity sheet entitled "My Best Trait" and have each student complete it by reading the sample story and writing his/her own story.

7. ***Independent Use:*** Ask students to identify positive traits about themselves that are related to their home environment. Ask them to write this skill in the form of a story and how the skill has benefited them. They are to bring the story to class to read and share within a week.

8. ***Continuation:*** The teacher will continue to point out the need for each student to like himself or herself as related situations arise.

CHILDREN'S LITERATURE

Do an author study of Gary Paulsen. Some good read-aloud books are *Hatchet* and *The River.* Go to the library to find information about the author who learned to overcome many hardships and became a writer of children's books.

Name _____ Date _____

MY BEST TRAIT

Write a story about something you like so much about yourself that you would like to give it to a newly created species. Make it as amusing as possible. When you have completed the story, illustrate it with a small drawing on the same paper.

Example: *Why I Gave Away the Perfect Toe*

Once upon a time in the land of Roads, the King asked for each person to select the thing he/she liked best about himself/herself. One little boy could not make up his mind. He didn't think he had anything exceptional. Suddenly, a huge monster began to chase the boy. He ran fast until he came to a high wall. There was no way to climb it. What could he do? He noticed a small hole in the wall. Carefully, he put his toe in the hole and, lo and behold, a ladder appeared on the wall. Then he knew what was special . . . his toe. His beautiful toe had saved his life.

Now write your story!

SOCIAL SKILL

Accepting the Consequences for Breaking the Rules

Behavioral Objective: The student will list an acceptable consequence for an inappropriate action.

Directed Lesson:

1. **Establish the Need:** Discuss with the class the purpose of the lesson. Say, **"When we do something wrong, we must also be willing to accept the consequences."**

2. **Introduction:** Teacher tells the following story:

   "Your mother told you to come in at 7:00 P.M. Well, you were so busy playing that it was 9:00 P.M. when you came in from outside. You must therefore be willing to accept the consequence for your misguided actions."

   Ask, **"What might be a consequence for staying out past time?"** Sample responses might be: not being able to go out to play for a day or two, no T.V. tonight, etc.

3. **Identify the Skill Components:** (List on the board.)

   1. Think about the situation.
   2. Think about your action(s).
   3. Admit you're wrong, and that you must accept the consequences.
   4. Apologize for your action(s).
   5. Take the consequences.

4. **Model the Skill:** Teacher presents the following situation to the class: **"A class report was due on Monday, but one student thought it was due Friday. The teacher had explained to all students that if they did not hand the report in on time, they would get a lower grade and a note would be sent home to their parents."** The teacher then models the behavior from the steps listed on the board.

5. **Behavioral Rehearsal:**

   A. **Selection:** Students volunteer to role play the following:

   B. **Role Play:**

   1. Principal talking to a student about not following proper bus rules. *Consequence:* bus referral and chart marked.

   2. Lunch attendant talking to student about not having lunch token. *Consequence:* must wait until everyone is served before getting a lunch.

71

    C. ***Completion:*** After each role play, reinforce correct behavior, identify inappropriate behaviors, and reenact role play with corrections. If there are no corrections, role play is complete.

    D. ***Reinforcers:*** Verbal praise, nonverbal approval, group reinforcement.

    E. ***Discussion:*** Discuss role play results.

6. ***Practice:*** Distribute copies of the following activity sheet, "Choosing a Consequence," and have students complete it in class. Discuss the information.

7. ***Independent Use:*** Have students write about situations at home which cause them to have to face the consequences. Students to share writings in class.

8. ***Continuation:*** Teacher should point out the need for this skill as related situations arise throughout the year.

Name _____ Date _____

CHOOSING A CONSEQUENCE

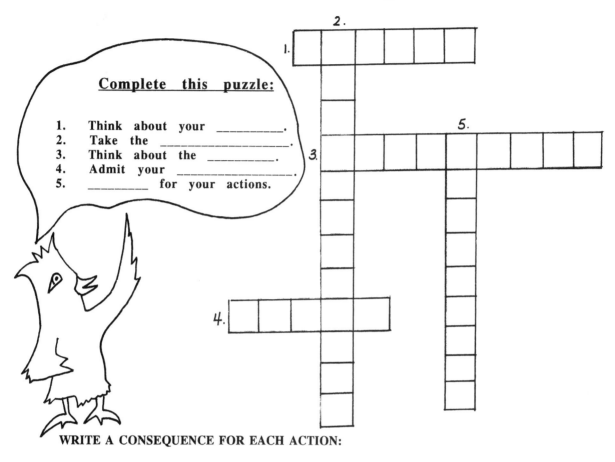

Complete this puzzle:

1. Think about your _____.
2. Take the _____.
3. Think about the _____.
4. Admit your _____.
5. _____ for your actions.

WRITE A CONSEQUENCE FOR EACH ACTION:

1. During an assembly, a student continued to talk after being warned.

_____

2. In the morning, a child picked up breakfast and threw it on the floor.

_____

3. Mother said to do the chores before playing, but you went out to play first.

_____

4. Your friend borrowed your crayons and lost them.

_____

5. A homework assignment was due. You didn't turn it in.

Lesson 22

SOCIAL SKILL

Accepting the Consequences for Inappropriate Behavior

Behavioral Objective: The student will admit what he/she had done, and accept the consequences without becoming defensive.

Directed Lesson:

1. **Establish the Need:** Review with the class why we should accept the consequences for what we do without becoming defensive. Ask: Why it is important for us to accept consequences in a nondefensive manner? What might happen if we don't accept consequences in a nondefensive way?

2. **Introduction:** Teacher reads the following story:

   "Mary was on her way home from school. She saw her friend Joanie who to her great surprise invited her to come over to her house to see her doll collection. Mary said she couldn't because her mother had told her to always come home first and ask for permission. Joanie convinced Mary to come on over anyway, because it wouldn't take long. The two girls played and had so much fun with the dolls that they forgot what time it was. Suddenly Mary remembered that she had to go home. On her way home, Mary was quite worried about what her mother was going to say or do to her. When Mary got home her mother was out on the front porch looking for her. Mary admitted her wrongdoing, and apologized for her actions. When her mother told her that she could not go out to play or watch T.V. for a week, Mary said, 'All right, Mother,' and went to her room."

   Have the students recall what Mary did, the consequences involved, and what she said to her mother.

3. **Identify the Skill Components:** (List on the board.)

   1. Think about what you did.
   2. Think about the consequences involved.
   3. Tell yourself that you did wrong, and you will accept the consequences.
   4. Apologize.

4. **Model the Skill:** Teacher shows the skill components in the following situation: In art class the student (played by the teacher) paints her nails instead of painting the picture. Choose a student to be the art teacher. *Consequence:* no art tomorrow and a phone call to the parents.

5. **Behavioral Rehearsal:**

   A. **Selection:** Students volunteer to role play the following.

B. ***Role Play:***

1. Your friend lets you hold his sunglasses. You put them on and trip, breaking the glasses. *Consequence:* pay for the glasses.

2. Playing in a game, you made the wrong move. Your team loses. *Consequence:* two extra days of practice ordered by the coach.

C. ***Completion:*** After each role play, reinforce correct behavior, identify inappropriate behaviors, and reenact role play with corrections. If there are no corrections, role play is complete.

D. ***Reinforcers:*** Verbal praise, nonverbal encouragement, group reinforcement.

E. ***Discussion:*** Discuss and review results of role play.

6. ***Practice:*** Distribute copies of the following activity sheet, "Truth and Consequence," for students to complete in class.

7. ***Independent Use:*** Have students keep a record of consequences they encountered and how they responded for a week.

8. ***Continuation:*** Teacher tells students, **"It is important for each one of us to treat other people the way we want them to treat us."**

Also, each classroom is a *team* and requires the cooperation of every class member.

Name _____ Date _____

TRUTH AND CONSEQUENCE

Directions: Record your actions and the consequences you received for one week. They could have occurred at home, at school, or with friends.

Monday	
Tuesday	
Wednesday	
Thursday	
Friday	

I hope you accepted the consequences without becoming defensive.

SOCIAL SKILL
Accepting Consequences Without Anger

Behavioral Objective: The student will accept the consequences without getting angry.

Directed Lesson:

1. ***Establish the Need:*** Students need to accept consequences so that the school and home environments can run smoothly. Students need to know how to apologize to maintain a healthy relationship.

2. ***Introduction:*** The teacher reads the Aesop's Fable entitled "The Fox and the Crow" to the class.

   "A fox once saw a crow sitting on a branch with a large piece of cheese in her mouth. Hungry for cheese, the sly fox said, 'Good day, Mistress Crow, what a fine bird you are. How black your feathers are. And what a well-shaped beak. You must have a wonderful singing voice.' The crow was so pleased with this extravagant praise that she opened her mouth to sound a hoarse 'Caw.' The cheese fell from her mouth and the fox snapped it up and ran away."

   What lesson do you think the Crow should have learned from this?

3. ***Identify the Skill Components:*** (List on the board before class.)

   1. Accept that you are wrong.
   2. Apologize.
   3. Accept the consequences.
   4. Show no verbal or nonverbal anger.

4. ***Model the Skill:*** The teacher will role play a situation in which he/she breaks the rules of a game and is not permitted to play again until the next time. Reinforce the concept that the rules of the game are not negotiable, and the challenge is to play by the rules.

5. ***Behavioral Rehearsal:***

   A. ***Selection:*** Teacher selects students for role play.

   B. ***Role Play:*** The students will tell of an incident where they did something wrong and had to accept a consequence. How did they react to the consequence?

   C. ***Completion:*** After each role play, reinforce correct behavior, identify inappropriate behaviors, and reenact role play with corrections. If there are no corrections, role play is complete.

D. ***Reinforcers:*** Material rewards, verbal praise, group reinforcement.

E. ***Discussion:*** Students discuss the need to accept consequences for inappropriate behaviors if society is to function properly. By choosing an inappropriate behavior, the person has to accept the consequences for the behavior.

6. ***Practice:*** Distribute copies of the following activity sheet, "Tell the Truth Interview," and complete it in the class.

7. ***Independent Use:*** Have students write a paragraph describing how they apologized for doing something they knew was wrong. Have the students bring this paragraph to class for discussion.

8. ***Continuation:*** The teacher reminds students that one sign of being "grown-up" is accepting responsibility for our actions without getting angry.

CHILDREN'S LITERATURE

Get a copy of *Aesop's Fables* from the library and read one story a day. Have students think about the lesson to be learned and how to apply it to life in school.

Name _____ Date _____

TELL THE TRUTH INTERVIEW

Choose a partner and fill in the following interview items:

Tell of an incident where you did something wrong and there was a consequence.

_____

_____

_____

_____

How did you react to the consequence?

_____

_____

_____

_____

Name of interviewer_____

Name of person interviewed_____

SOCIAL SKILL
Responding Calmly to Failure

Behavioral Objective: The student will learn to control his/her reaction to failure and the consequences that go with it.

Directed Lesson:

1. **Establish the Need:** If students remain calm, then they will be able to plan and think logically about what to do next.

2. **Introduction:** The teacher describes the situation to the class.

> **"One afternoon, Mike wanted to play Monopoly. His brother couldn't play because he had to do his homework. His mother was busy doing housework and cooking dinner. His father was at work. Mike can't find anyone to play Monopoly with him. What should he do now?"**

   Have the class tell what they think Mike should do next.

3. **Identify the Skill Components:** (List on board before class.)

   1. Decide *if* you failed. (Did you fail because you did not get what you wanted?)
   2. Decide why you failed.
   3. Avoid making the same mistakes by planning ahead.

4. **Model the Skill:** The teacher will role play a situation in which he/she will be unable to complete an activity and will accept the consequences.

5. **Behavioral Rehearsal:**

   A. **Selection:** The teacher will select two students for each role play.

   B. **Role Play:** Students will use the role plays listed below.

   1. Did not win an art poster contest.
   2. Did not earn the grade expected on a test.
   3. Failed a driving test.
   4. Failed to complete chores and therefore did not get allowance.

   C. **Completion:** After each role play, reinforce correct behavior, identify inappropriate behaviors, and reenact role play with corrections. If there are no corrections, role play is complete.

   D. **Reinforcers:** Material rewards, verbal praise, group reinforcement.

E. ***Discussion:*** Students will discuss what it means to fail to accomplish something or to win and how they should react to either situation.

6. ***Practice:*** Distribute copies of the following activity sheet, "What Is Failure?" and have students complete it together in class.

7. ***Independent Use:*** The student will find a newspaper clipping or television story that illustrates failure with a consequence. This assignment is due next week to be discussed in class.

8. ***Continuation:*** The teacher should continue to point out that the best way to respond to failure is to find out why it happened and how to avoid making the same mistake.

Name _____ Date _____

"WHAT IS FAILURE?"

* *

Directions: Write a paragraph describing the *difference* between failure to reach a goal that you set for yourself, and failure to comply with rules for which there are real consequences. Explain both by using an example.

* *

_____

_____

_____

_____

_____

_____

_____

_____

_____

_____

_____

* *

SOCIAL SKILL

Accepting Consequences for Inappropriate Behavior

Behavioral Objective: Students will accept deserved consequences without complaining for behavior that is unacceptable.

Directed Lesson:

1. **Establish the Need:** Review school and class rules that deal with accepting consequences for inappropriate behaviors. Emphasize that accepting consequences will cause a more orderly environment and lessen the frustrations for students in their daily experiences in school and home. By mastering this skill, students will gain the respect of staff and peers. This will increase their popularity in all social situations.

2. **Introduction:** The teacher tells a story about a man/student/boy who was very unhappy because no one liked him. The reason was that he always made excuses and was never willing to admit that he had made a mistake. If punished, he always became angry and was abusive to everyone he encountered. Finally, he began using the skill component steps. To his surprise, they worked! He was amazed that everyone seemed to be more tolerant. He was much happier.

3. **Identify the Skill Components:** (List on board before class.)

   1. Think about what was done wrong.
   2. Decide what role you played in making a mistake.
   3. Decide what you can do or say to apologize.
   4. Apologize sincerely.
   5. Accept consequence without complaints.
   6. Determine how to prevent mistakes in the future.

4. **Model the Skill:** Teacher will model the skill by playing "Simon Says." Teacher asks a group of students to help and appoint a leader. Teacher does not follow the rules of the game and has to drop out of the game as a consequence.

5. **Behavioral Rehearsal:**

   A. **Selection:** Teacher selects five pairs of students to role play. One student will not follow the rules, the other will determine the consequences.

   B. **Role Play:** Suggestions for student role plays are listed on the activity sheet. The teacher might hand out a card with the role play written on it for each pair of students.

    C. ***Completion:*** After each role play, reinforce correct behavior, identify inappropriate behavior, and reenact role play with corrections. If there are no corrections, role play is complete.

    D. ***Reinforcers:*** Verbal praise, nonverbal praise (i.e., smile, pat, handshake), written notes of approval, and note of improved social behavior on the report card.

    E. ***Discussion:*** Have a discussion after the role play to reinforce skill steps. Ask students to describe how it felt to role play both sides of the situation.

       Students can brainstorm and list many ways that rules enable traffic to move smoothly (eg., red/green lights, stop sign, one-way traffic, pedestrians only, no parking, etc.). The rules are made to keep order on the streets and to promote safety for drivers and pedestrians.

6. ***Practice:*** Distribute copies of the activity sheet entitled "Write the Consequence" and have students complete it in class and hand it in.

7. ***Independent Use:*** Send home copies of the following "Letter to Home" explaining this approach. Ask parents to sign the letter indicating that their child is using the same method at home.

8. ***Continuation:*** Teachers should point out the need for appropriate behavior as related situations arise.

Name _____ Date _____

WRITE THE CONSEQUENCE

Directions: Write what you feel would be an appropriate consequence for the misbehaviors listed below:

MISBEHAVIOR	**CONSEQUENCE**
1. FIGHTING ON THE BUS............	....
2. FIGHTING AT THE BUS STOP......	....
3. FORGETTING HOMEWORK..........	....
4. SLOPPY HOMEWORK	....
5. USING PROFANITY.............	....
6. TALKING BACK TO ADULT........	....
7. FIGHTING IN SCHOOL..........	....
8. FIGHTING ON THE WAY TO SCHOOL	....
9. DISOBEYING LUNCHROOM AIDES...	....
10. FIBBING ABOUT A STUDENT......	....

Write four things you can do in learning to accept consequences:

1.

2.

3.

4.

SHAPE UP. Select two things to work on from the Misbehavior List.

Date: _____

LETTER TO HOME

Dear _____:

I am learning to accept the consequences when I break the rules of our school and class-room. By learning to accept the consequences for my actions, I am showing that I know how to treat other people as I wish to be treated by them and can behave like a responsible person.

When I misbehave in class, my teacher asks me to write down what I did and what I think would be an appropriate consequence for it. I need you to help me use the same method at home.

Misbehavior | Consequence

Please sign this note so that I can return it to my teacher. Thank you!

Your signature: _____

Parent/Guardian signature: _____ Date: _____

ACCEPTING CONSEQUENCES   Lesson 26

SOCIAL SKILL
Using Problem-Solving Skills

Behavioral Objective: The student will identify consequences that are difficult for him/her to accept and apply problem-solving skills to change the offending behavior or accept the consequences more easily.

Directed Lesson:

1. ***Establish the Need:*** Everyone (from a tiny baby learning which objects are safe to play with, to a senior citizen learning which foods he/she can no longer eat) lives with consequences. Some are positive—these bring satisfaction. Some are negative—these are hard to accept. Consequences that are really hard to accept may seem HARSH or punishing. (You splurge on a huge meal "just for once" and the next day your scale punishes you mightily!) Consequences may be UNEXPECTED: The student who leaves his bike out is surprised when it is stolen. Finally, consequences may be unacceptable because the behaviors that caused them are VERY HARD TO CHANGE: You know you should go to bed early so you can think the next day, But your FAVORITE show comes on late at night. The problem of accepting consequences is a universal one and we will study it today.

2. ***Introduction:*** Guide students to acquire about man-made and natural consequences due to behavior, and to determine which consequences are difficult and which are easy for them to accept. Distribute copies of the following activity sheet, entitled "Consequences of Behavior," and complete this as a group activity.

3. ***Identify the Skill Components:*** (List on the board before class.)
    1. Identify unacceptable consequences.
    2. Apply problem solving skills (see activity sheet "Problem Solving").
    3. Try to change the problem behavior.
    4. Understand and accept the consequences.

4. ***Model the Skill:*** Teacher shares with the class a consequence which is difficult to accept; namely, that the leaves on her plants have turned brown because she forgot to water them. Next, teacher models the six steps in the problem-solving process (see activity sheet "Problem Solving") and decides on a solution. Note that one alternative is not to change the problem behavior, but to reject the consequence of having dried out plants (i.e., buying artificial ones).

5. ***Behavioral Rehearsal:***
    A. ***Selection:*** All students will be included.
    B. ***Role Play:*** Give students copies of the following "Problem Solving" activity sheet and have each student complete it showing, as the teacher did, a solution to the problem.

87

    C. ***Completion:*** After each role play, reinforce correct behavior, identify inappropriate behaviors, and reenact role play with corrections. If there are no corrections, role play is complete.

    D. ***Reinforcers:*** Verbal praise, material award, recognition. The students should be encouraged to help each other to solve problems by offering ideas, understanding, and encouragement.

    E. ***Discussion:*** Evaluate the success of solutions in small groups, through a private written assignment, or as a class-sharing process.

6. ***Practice:*** Use the two activity sheets accompanying this lesson to give students further practice in applying problem-solving skills.

7. ***Independent Use:*** Have students make a cartoon strip about an inappropriate behavior and its consequence. This behavior should have occurred at home, or outside school.

8. ***Continuation:*** The teacher tells students that they have the power to change their own behavior if they cannot accept the consequences.

Name _____ Date _____

CONSEQUENCES OF BEHAVIOR

Directions: Use the following chart to list ten Behaviors and Consequences. On the rating scale, determine the level of **ease** or **difficulty** in accepting consequences. The first one is done for you.

BEHAVIOR	NATURAL CONSEQUENCE	MAN-MADE CONSEQUENCE	RATING 1 - 5 (e) (d)
stay up late	sleepy	get into fight	4
eating too much			
animal run out			
drugs			

Name _____ Date _____

Problem Solving

1. State the "problem behavior": _____

_____.

2. BRAINSTORM possible causes for behavior:

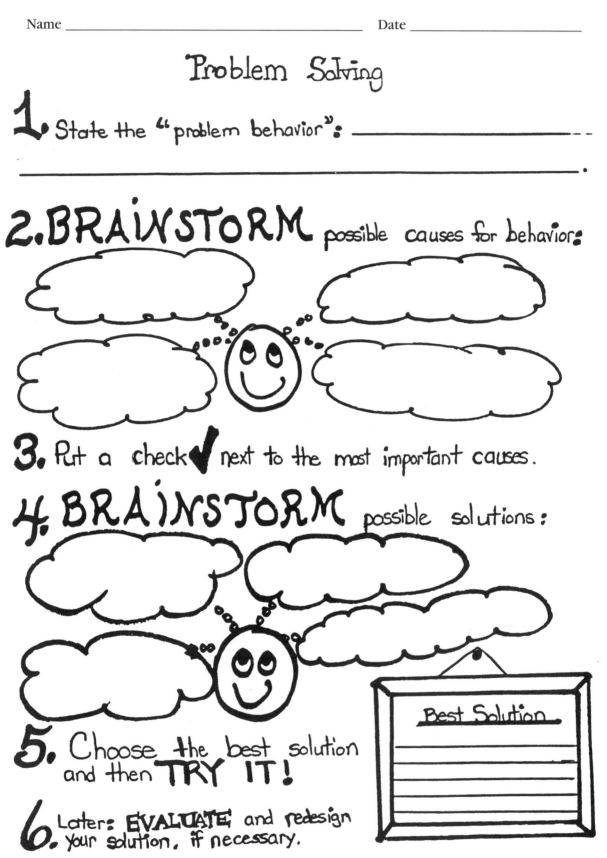

3. Put a check ✔ next to the most important causes.

4. BRAINSTORM possible solutions:

5. Choose the best solution and then **TRY IT!**

Best Solution

6. Later: **EVALUATE** and redesign your solution, if necessary.

SOCIAL SKILL

Refusing Requests in a Positive Manner

Behavioral Objective: The student will politely refuse another student's request to join him in a game before his work is finished.

Directed Lesson:

1. **Establish the Need:** Teacher will discuss with the students that sometimes we have to refuse requests made by others. In order to avoid conflict we have to learn to refuse others' requests in a positive and polite manner.

2. **Introduction:** The teacher will ask a student to pretend he wants to borrow something from the teacher—colored markers, for example. Teacher will say **"Mary I know you like to color with the markers. I'm sorry but you cannot use them now. I told Greg he could use them."** Have students identify the behavior of the teacher.

3. **Identify the Skill Components:** (List on the board.)

    1. Think about the consequence of accepting or refusing a request.

    2. Make a decision if you can accept a request.

    3. If not, tell the person "no" politely and in a positive manner.

    4. Tell the person why you can't do what he/she asked.

4. **Model the Skill:** Teacher will model the skill by refusing a student's request to play a game before the work is finished and then reverse the roles by having a student politely refuse the same request by the teacher.

5. **Behavioral Rehearsal:**

    A. **Selection:** Ask for three pairs of volunteers.

    B. **Role Play:** Teacher will give students role playing situations which will enable them to practice the behavior.

        1. Student asks another to borrow a pencil.

        2. Student asks another to go to the store with him/her after school.

        3. Student asks another to do his/her homework.

    C. **Completion:** After each role play, reinforce correct behavior, identify inappropriate behaviors, and reenact role play with corrections. If there are no corrections, role play is complete.

    D. **Reinforcers:** Material rewards, verbal praise, nonverbal expression of approval (i.e., smile, pat, hug), group reinforcement.

    E. ***Discussion:*** Discuss how well students followed skill components.

6. ***Practice:*** Assign students a writing assignment. Tell them they may choose someone to play a game with when they have completed the assignment. Tell students to politely refuse if they have not yet completed the assignment. (Students must complete the assignment to the teacher's satisfaction.)

7. ***Independent Use:*** Have parents ask students to do things that they have to refuse. Check to see that students refuse in a friendly manner.

8. ***Continuation:*** The teacher should remind students that it pays to be polite and friendly when they have to refuse another person's request.

CHILDREN'S LITERATURE

Isaacs, Anne. *Swamp Angel.* Illustrated by Paul O. Zelinsky. NY: Dutton, 1994.

SOCIAL SKILL
Applying Decision-Making Skills

Behavioral Objective: The student will stop and think, then use appropriate decision-making skills.

Directed Lesson:

1. *Establish the Need:* This skill is necessary for a successful social life now and in the future.

2. *Introduction:* Teacher reads the following situation to class:

   "One afternoon at school, Miss Smith was teaching a social studies lesson on why we have laws. James was very anxious to make a comment. Miss Smith ended the discussion before James had a chance to make his point. James became very upset."

   How should James resolve the problem?

3. *Identify the Skill Components:* (List on board before class.)

   1. Stop being upset.
   2. Start to think.
   3. Relax.
   4. Decide how to keep your self-control.
   5. Think about what you can do.
   6. Make a decision.

4. *Model the Skill:* Teacher will model the skill by showing the correct response to an upsetting situation.

5. *Behavioral Rehearsal:*

   A. *Selection:* Teacher selects four pairs of students for role plays.

   B. *Role Play:* Using the role play suggestions listed below, each student will tell how they would react to the situation.

      1. A student takes your pencil and looses it.
      2. Your parents won't let you ride your bike.
      3. You must baby-sit your brother or sister.
      4. You didn't finish your math assignment.

    C. ***Completion:*** After each role play, reinforce correct behavior, identify inappropriate behaviors, and reenact role play with corrections. If there are no corrections, role play is complete.

    D. ***Reinforcers:*** Material rewards, verbal praise, group reinforcement, nonverbal expression of approval.

    E. ***Discussion:*** Students discuss results and consequences of making appropriate and inappropriate decisions.

6. ***Practice:*** Distribute copies of the following activity sheet entitled "What's Your Reaction?" Have students complete the activity and share their answers in class.

7. ***Independent Use:*** Give students copies of the following "Reaction Sheet" to take home to their parents.

8. ***Continuation:*** Teacher will remind students of the need to apply decision-making skills whenever they are in a situation that requires it.

Name _____ Date _____

WHAT'S YOUR REACTION?

☞ ☞ ☞ ☞ ☞ ☞ ☞ ☞ ☞ ☞ ☞ ☞ ☞ ☞ ☞ ☞

Directions: After reading each situation below, write an (A) appropriate (B) inappropriate reaction in the spaces provided.

☞ ☞ ☞ ☞ ☞ ☞ ☞ ☞ ☞ ☞ ☞ ☞ ☞ ☞ ☞ ☞

1. A student takes something you like very much and loses it.

   A. _____

   B. _____

2. Your parents won't let you go to a concert.

   A. _____

   B. _____

3. You want to go to the park but you must baby-sit for your brother.

   A. _____

   B. _____

4. You didn't do your homework but your friend did.

   A. _____

   B. _____

☞ ☞ ☞ ☞ ☞ ☞ ☞ ☞ ☞ ☞ ☞ ☞ ☞ ☞ ☞ ☞

Name _____ Date _____

REACTION SHEET

Dear Parents,

Ask your child to complete all homework assignments for a week, and record your child's reaction on this sheet. Examples of your child's reaction might be: showed eagerness, complained, incomplete, worked carefully, etc. This sheet is due at the beginning of next week.

Sincerely,

_____

(Teacher's Signature)

DAYS	Monday	Tuesday	Wednesday	Thursday	Friday
REACTION					

_____

(Parent's Signature)

SOCIAL SKILL
Maintaining Self-Control

Behavioral Objective: The student will stop and think, then use appropriate decision-making skills.

Directed Lesson:

1. ***Establish the Need:*** This skill is necessary for the student to have a successful social life now and in the future, and to avoid problem situations.

2. ***Introduction:*** The teacher reads the following situation:

   "Jack Smiley and Joseph Toughly were walking home from school one day. Joseph decided to play tag with Jack, but he punched him too hard. What do you think Jack should do so that he doesn't lose control?"

   Discuss with the class what they think Jack should do.

3. ***Identify the Skill Components:*** (List on board before class.)

   1. Stop being upset.
   2. Start to think.
   3. Relax.
   4. Decide what to do to keep self-control.
   5. Think about the different choices you have.
   6. Make a choice.

4. ***Model the Skill:*** Teacher role plays a situation which forces him/her to stop and think to keep from losing control and to relax in order to be able to make a good decision.

5. ***Behavioral Rehearsal:***

   A. ***Selection:*** Teacher selects students for each role play.

   B. ***Role Play:*** Using the role play suggestions listed below, each student will tell how he/she would react to the situation.

   — A student rips up your only "A" paper.

   — Your mother insists that you wash dishes before going to school.

   — You forgot to return your overdue library books.

C. ***Completion:*** After each role play, reinforce correct behavior, identify inappropriate behaviors, and reenact role play with corrections. If there are no corrections, role play is complete.

D. ***Reinforcers:*** Material rewards, verbal praise, group reinforcement.

E. ***Discussion:*** Students will discuss the benefits of maintaining self-control and the negative consequences if they fail to do so.

6. ***Practice:*** Distribute copies of the following activity sheet entitled "Self-Control Reaction Sheet" to students and complete it together in class.

7. ***Independent Use:*** The student will tell one incident where he/she had to use the skill steps.

8. ***Continuation:*** Teacher reminds students of the importance of self-control in getting along with each other as related situations arise.

Name _____ Date _____

SELF-CONTROL REACTION SHEET

SKILL STEPS:
   ✓ 1. Stop to think.
   ✓ 2. Decide if you are losing self-control.
   ✓ 3. Think about your choices.
   ✓ 4. Relax.
   ✓ 5. Make a choice.

ACCORDING TO THE SKILL STEPS LISTED ABOVE, HOW SHOULD LINDA REACT TO THE FOLLOWING SITUATION? WRITE YOUR RESPONSE ON THE LINES PROVIDED.

Linda wants to be in the school choir but there is a problem. Her mother will not bring her to the evening choir programs at school. Linda is upset and refuses to join another choir at her church which would allow her to sing at other occasions.

_____

_____

_____

_____

_____

SOCIAL SKILL
Remaining Calm Under Stress

Behavioral Objective: The student will use strategies for remaining calm under stress.

Directed Lesson:

1. **Establish the Need:** Anyone can lose control and become angry, but it takes a strong person to maintain self-control during stressful situations. Emphasize that it is important to maintain self-control so that a person does not face unnecessary, unpleasant consequences.

2. **Introduction:** Discuss with the class that many crimes are committed because people do not know how to remain calm under stress. Some people do not intentionally set out to hurt others, but they become angry and do not know how to handle the situation. Even if others are at fault, serious upsets can be prevented, if we can exercise self-control.

3. **Identify the Skill Components:** Write the following skill components on the board before class.

    1. Stop and think about the situation causing stress.
    2. Count to ten silently while trying to remain calm.
    3. Decide what has upset you and why.
    4. Relax.
    5. Decide what you will do next.
        A. Leave the situation.
        B. Tell the person who has caused the situation how you feel.
        C. Talk to a neutral person.
        D. Write your feelings to someone (yourself).
        E. Record your feelings on a cassette tape.

4. **Model the Skill:** Teacher will model the skill by following the skill steps to solve a simulated situation in which a student has caused the teacher to become upset (e.g., student has taken the teacher's attendance book from her desk).

5. **Behavior Rehearsal:**

    A. **Selection:** Ask for six pairs of students to role play.
    B. **Role Play:** Have students role play some of the following situations:

        1. Someone bumps into you and causes you to drop your books. He/she does not offer to pick them up.

100

2. You have been tripped while taking your assignment to the teacher.

3. You have tried hard to do your very best, but the teacher demands more.

4. You had hoped to become class president, but you lost the election to someone you feel is not a good choice.

5. While you are finishing your art project, someone accidentally bumps your desk and causes your hand to slip. Your art project is ruined.

6. You have been punched and called names on the school bus. You have been told not to fight or call names. You try hard, but you are punched again. The bus driver cannot see what is going on.

C. **Completion:** After each role play, reinforce correct behavior, identify inappropriate behaviors, and reenact role play with corrections. If there are no corrections, role play is complete.

D. **Reinforcers:** Verbal praise, self-control charts, and "Stay Cool Badges."

E. **Discussion:** Discuss why it is important to remain calm under stress. How do we stay calm? What can happen if we do not use self-control?

6. **Practice:** Distribute copies of the following "A Trying Situation" activity sheet and ask each student to write about the most trying situation he/she has faced. Then tell how he/she was able to use his/her self-control to handle the situation. Remember to include the five skill steps used in reaching this solution.

7. **Independent Use:** Have students log the number of times he/she has been upset during the week and the number of times he/she has kept his/her temper under control. Differentiate between home and school. Have students discuss these logs in class.

8. **Continuation:** Teacher should continue pointing out the need for this skill as related situations arise.

Name _____ Date _____

A TRYING SITUATION

Directions: Describe the most trying situation you have faced. Then, tell how you resolved the situation using the 5 skill components for remaining calm under stress.

*Situation:*_____

_____

_____

_____

_____

_____

_____

How I Handled the Situation:

1. _____

2. _____

3. _____

4. _____

5. _____

SOCIAL SKILL

Practicing Self-Restraint

Behavioral Objective: Student will be able to state and to demonstrate alternative behaviors in situations where she/he typically loses self-control.

Directed Lesson:

1. **Establish the Need:** Students must understand that they must use self-restraint many times each day if they want to avoid unpleasant consequences.

2. **Introduction:** Teacher reads about situations encountered by two students.

   "Consider the case of Janie. She is usually a model of self-restraint. She expresses her feelings appropriately when she's angry, and does not swear. She tries not to eat too much candy . . . but alas, poor Janie has a difficult time when it comes to keeping secrets. She blurts out even her best friend's private conversation.

   Consider the case of Joey, who is usually a paragon of self-control. He is so patient with his baby brother, he doesn't even lose his temper when the little boy colors all over his homework! But . . . when it comes to saving money, he just can't control himself. The money seems to make his fingers itch until he has spent every last nickel! Both Janie and Joey have a problem, a problem common to each of us to some degree, the problem of inadequate self-control."

3. **Identify the Skill Components:** (List on the board before class.)

   1. Identify situations where self-control is needed.
   2. Choose one situation of great concern.
   3. Think of alternative ways of behaving in such a situation.
   4. Practice self-restrained behaviors.

4. **Model the Skill:** Have teacher put himself/herself in the place of Janie. The teacher (playing Janie) shows how she can solve her problem of lack of self-control for keeping secrets. Use the skill steps. Can you help to think of alternative behaviors she could practice? What should she think to herself when she is told a secret? What can she do to conquer the urge to divulge secrets? (List ideas.) Teacher models the ideas of thinking before she acts and considering the consequences of her behavior.

5. **Behavioral Rehearsal:**

   A. **Selection:** Teacher asks for one volunteer. The volunteer calls on several students of his/hers choosing to be in the role play.

B. ***Role Play:*** Teacher lists on board various situations students name as problems for self-controlled behavior (e.g., when someone cuts in front of the lunch line). The class observes as a group, and:

    a. votes on the problem of greatest concern from list on board.

    b. brainstorms alternative ways to the problem behavior.

    c. selects, by voting or informal agreement, the best alternative behavior.

    d. enacts the situation, using the alternative behavior.

C. ***Completion:*** After each role play, reinforce correct behavior, identify inappropriate behaviors, and reenact role play with corrections. If there are no corrections, role play is complete.

D. ***Reinforcers:*** Reinforce verbally the positive actions of the group.

E. ***Discussion:*** Have the class discuss how well the group role played and selected the best alternative behavior for keeping self-control.

6. ***Practice:*** Have the class select a problem that causes loss of self-control which arises often in the classroom. Suggest alternative behaviors that can be used to counter act losing self-control. Divide the class into two groups. One group will practice the suggested behaviors, and the other group will observe and evaluate. Have the groups reverse roles. Discuss their observations.

7. ***Independent Use:*** Students will write down situations when they had to use self-control at home and will report their findings to the class at the end of the week.

8. ***Continuation:*** Teachers should continue pointing out the need for this skill as related situations arise.

Teachers should stress the importance of self-control in all interactions with one another.

GOAL SETTING

SOCIAL SKILL
Learning to Set a Goal

Behavioral Objective: The student will learn how to set a goal.

Directed Lesson:

1. ***Establish the Need:*** Teacher will discuss reason for all class members to arrive at school on time, e.g., you might miss something important. There are school rules and consequences for arriving late, etc.

2. ***Introduction:*** Begin the discussion by describing some of the benefits students will reap from learning this skill. Also discuss the consequences of not learning this skill.

3. ***Identify the Skill Components:*** (List on the board.)

    1. Decide on the skill you want to achieve.
    2. Decide on steps needed to reach the goal.
    3. Take each step needed to reach the goal.
    4. Reward yourself when the goal is reached.

4. ***Model the Skill:*** Teacher tells students steps he/she took to arrive at school on time. Have students tell what they do to get to school on time.

5. ***Behavioral Rehearsal:***

    A. ***Selection:*** Select students for role play.

    B. ***Role Play:***
    1. Student should know what time he/she is required to be in class.
    2. Student should decide what time he/she needs to leave home to arrive at school on time.
    3. Student should write the time down as a reminder.
    4. Student rewards self when goal is reached (self-praise).

    C. ***Completion:*** The student should be given some type of reward every time he/she arrives on time.

    D. ***Reinforcers:*** Material rewards, verbal praise, nonverbal expression of approval (i.e., smile, pat, hug), group reinforcement.

    E. ***Discussion:*** Students will discuss the benefits of arriving on time and observation of role play.

6. ***Practice:*** Students should make a chart and keep records for two weeks of how many times they arrive at school on time. Teacher will give them a sticker, or star if they arrive on time every day of the two weeks.

7. ***Independent Use:*** Parents will aid student in getting to school on time. Parents can keep a chart telling the time the student leaves each morning.

8. ***Continuation:*** Teachers should continue pointing out the need for setting goals, then working to achieve them, as related situations arise.

SOCIAL SKILL
Setting Successive Goals

Behavioral Objective: The students will set two weekly goals, one monthly goal, and one semester goal.

Directed Lesson:

1. **Establish the Need:** The students should be responsible for setting goals and reaching them. Setting goals gives the student a target to try to reach and builds self-control and internal motivation.

2. **Introduction:** The teacher should read the following story:

   "Once there were two boys, Juan and Jose. Juan always seemed to get his work done and have free time. Jose always seemed to be in a rush to do this or that task and never seemed to have time to relax. Juan always decided what he had to do or wanted to do and figured out a plan to get his jobs done in the order in which they had to be completed. Jose always worked on what he was interested in at the moment no matter when the work had to be done. (1) Why was Juan successful? (2) Why was Jose always rushed? (3) Which plan do you think was better? Why?"

3. **Identify the Skill Components:** (List on board before class.)

   1. Think about things you need to do at school and at home to reach your goals.
   2. Decide which things can be done on a weekly, monthly, and semester basis.
   3. Make sure you set goals you can reach.
   4. Choose and make a list of two weekly, one monthly, and one semester goal.

4. **Model the Skill:** Teacher will list suggestions students give for various things that need to be done in school or at home and some goals for the class. Have the class review goals to see if they are goals that can be reached.

5. **Behavioral Rehearsal:**

   A. **Selection:** Teacher selects four students to role play.

   B. **Role Play:** Each student follows skill steps to set two weekly, one monthly, and one semester goal.

   C. **Completion:** After each role play, reinforce correct behavior, identify inappropriate behaviors, and reenact role play with corrections. If there are no corrections, role play is complete.

    D. ***Reinforcers:*** Verbal and written praise, group reinforcement.

    E. ***Discussion:*** Students will discuss goals selected and problems connected with reaching them and give favorable comments on each of the role plays.

6. ***Practice:*** Distribute copies of the following activity sheet, "Setting Goals," and have students complete it together in class.

7. ***Independent Use:*** Using the following activity sheet entitled "Weekly Goals Chart," the students will keep track of goals that were achieved. If they have more than two weekly goals planned, they should use the back of the chart for the additional goal(s).

8. ***Continuation:*** Teacher tells students that they will be amazed and pleased with how much they can accomplish when they learn to set and reach goals.

Name _____ Date _____

SETTING GOALS

Skill Steps:

1. First think about things that you need to do at school and at home to reach your goals.

2. Decide which things can be done on a *weekly, monthly,* and *semester* basis. Make sure these are goals you can reach.

3. Make a list of the weekly, monthly, and semester goals.

* *

You are to set two weekly goals, one monthly goal, and one semester goal. Some examples are: cleaning your room, chores, homework, visiting the library, book reports, and coming to school daily. You will have a checklist for the goals, some of which will be checked by the teacher, others which will be checked by your parents.

Weekly Goal #1 _____

_____

Weekly Goal #2 _____

_____

Monthly Goal _____

_____

Semester Goal _____

_____

* *

Name _____ Date _____

WEEKLY GOALS CHART

Put a check mark (✓) for each day that you work on your goal:

Weekly Goal #1

Week of:	Monday	Tuesday	Wednesday	Thursday	Friday	Saturday	✓

Weekly Goal #2

Week of:	Monday	Tuesday	Wednesday	Thursday	Friday	Saturday	✓

How am I doing? ✓ ✓ ✓

Keep at it!

SOCIAL SKILL

Setting and Achieving Goals

Behavioral Objective: The student will be able to set appropriate goals and apply himself/herself toward achieving them.

Directed Lesson:

1. **Establish the Need:** Discuss with the class that it is necessary to set and meet reasonable goals to function well in school and life. It is also important to see how well you are managing your tasks.

2. **Introduction:** Give students a timed test on math facts. Relate the importance of math fact mastery to success. Point out that memorizing math facts can become a challenge. Review the process of setting a goal and challenging yourself to meet that goal within a certain time. This can be a kind of internal competition and a source of satisfaction.

3. **Identify the Skill Components:** (List on board before class.)

   1. Set a goal that is neither too hard nor too easy.
   2. Write a plan for how you will achieve that goal.
   3. Apply yourself with real effort.
   4. Evaluate how well you did.

4. **Model the Skill:** The teacher shows a sample math fact test which can be done with 65% accuracy in two minutes. The teacher illustrates, with help from the class, the setting of a goal for accuracy improvement that is neither too ambitious nor too simple. Next the teacher illustrates the various ways that she/he can improve, e.g., writing and stating facts, using flash cards, or reviewing facts. The teacher will set a time limit when a new facts test is given.

5. **Behavioral Rehearsal:**

   A. **Selection:** Teacher selects five students to role play.

   B. **Role Play:** Ask class to decide on individual goals and have them set up a plan for reaching those goals. Have the five students share their goals and their plans for achieving them.

   C. **Completion:** After each role play, reinforce correct behavior, identify inappropriate behaviors, and reenact role play with corrections. If there are no corrections, role play is complete.

   D. **Reinforcers:** Verbal praise, achievement award, and good feelings for accomplished goals.

   E. ***Discussion:*** Discuss how well the role plays were done. Evaluate whether each student used the skill steps and whether the class feels the goals were reasonable. Is the process adequate?

6. ***Practice:*** Use the same process in subsequent math fact drill lessons. After the students begin to demonstrate skill in setting a goal in math, assign each student the task of setting goals in another area of their academic life: completing the reading of a library book within a given span of time, making up some work missed due to illness, being well-behaved for one day or week, undertaking a science project to show the class that they can do it.

7. ***Independent Use:*** Students will set a goal to complete a task outside the school. It must be completed in a specified time period. The students will report to the class on their successes and disappointments.

8. ***Continuation:*** Teachers should point out the importance of setting and meeting appropriate goals in all areas of life.

CHILDREN'S LITERATURE

Lowry, Lois. *Attaboy, Sam.* Illustrated by Diane DeGroat, NY: Houghton-Mifflin, 1992.

SOCIAL SKILL
Finishing Tasks on Time

Behavioral Objective: When assigned a task to complete in a reasonable time period, the student will finish on time.

Directed Lesson:

1. **Establish the Need:** Discuss with students the importance of completing assignments within a given amount of time; i.e., to allow time for other subjects or things of interest to the student, grade, etc. In some cases completion of a task is required at a given time, because further action will depend on the outcome of the task.

2. **Introduction:**

   1. Teacher will discuss the needs and rewards gained by those who complete their assignment on time.

   2. Teacher and class will discuss the appropriate things one needs to do in order to complete an assignment on time.

   3. Teacher and class discuss some of the inappropriate behaviors that cause students not to complete assignments on time.

   4. Teacher explains why the student should demonstrate the appropriate behavior of completing an assignment on time. Consequences are discussed.

   5. **Modeling:** The teacher will give a hypothetical situation describing a boy who didn't complete his work because he was talking and playing with friends.

   6. The student practices the appropriate behavior under the direction of the teacher. (Students are given a situation to role play.)

   7. **Feedback:** The teacher gives students both negative and positive feedback on their role play.

   8. **Feedback:** Students give feedback on how they felt, if they need to make changes in what they've learned.

   9. **Positive reinforcement:** The teacher verbally praises students for participating.

3. **Identify the Skill Components:** (List on the board.)

   1. Listen to the instruction.

   2. Follow directions given

   3. Have an understanding of subject matter.

   4. Avoid distractions.

   5. Use self-discipline to stay on task.

113

4. ***Model the Skill:***

   A. The teacher will orally give a hypothetical situation in which a boy didn't complete his work because he was talking and playing.

   B. Students will analyze the situation and come up with a way to correct the problem.

5. ***Behavioral Rehearsal:***

   A. ***Selection:*** Students volunteer to role play.

   B. ***Role Play:*** Use the following situations.

      - Students will role play a situation in which a boy doesn't complete his work because he chose to talk and play.

      - A second group of students will role play a situation where a student completed his work in a given amount of time because he ignored others who were talking and playing.

   C. ***Completion:*** After each role play, reinforce correct behavior, identify inappropriate behaviors, and reenact role play with corrections. If there are no corrections, role play is complete.

   D. ***Reinforcers:*** Material rewards, verbal praise, nonverbal praise.

   E. ***Discussion:*** Students will discuss the consequences in regard to both situations.

6. ***Practice:*** Distribute copies of the following two activity sheets, "On Task" and "Completing Assignment," for students to take home, complete, and return to school after they have been signed by their parent(s).

7. ***Independent Use:*** Ask parents to monitor their child's homework, making sure the task is completed in a given amount of time.

8. ***Continuation:*** Teachers should continue pointing out the need for this skill as related situations arise.

   Bring in a clock. Set it on a student's desk for five minutes to see how much work the student can accomplish during this time. Then, move the clock to another student's desk for the same purpose. Keep the clock moving.

ON TASK

Write the completed task subject under the date after you completed ALL assignments.

	M	*T*	*W*	*Th*	*F*
Dates					
Tasks					
Dates					
Tasks					
Dates					
Tasks					
Dates					
Tasks					
Dates					
Tasks					

Signatures:

Student _____

Teacher _____

Parent _____

Name _____ Date _____

COMPLETING ASSIGNMENTS

Make a list of things you must do to get your work done on time.

_____

_____

_____

_____

_____

_____

_____

Did you complete your assignment on time? _____

(Why or why not?) _____

_____

_____

_____

_____

_____

_____

Parent's Signature _____

COMPLETING ASSIGNMENTS   Lesson 36

SOCIAL SKILL
An Assigned Task

Behavioral Objective: When assigned a task at his/her mastery level, the student will work on it until it is completed.

Directed Lesson:

1. ***Establish the Need:*** Discuss with students the importance of completing assignments (improving grades, feeling good about oneself, etc.).

2. ***Introduction:***

    1. Teacher will discuss the needs and rewards gained by those who complete their assignments.

    2. Teacher and class will discuss the appropriate work habits students should have in order to complete an assignment successfully.

    3. Teacher and class discuss some of the inappropriate behaviors that cause students not to complete assignments.

    4. Teacher explains why students should demonstrate the appropriate behavior of completing an assignment. Consequences are discussed (your grade is affected).

3. ***Identify the Skill Components:*** (List on board.)

    1. Listen to instructions.

    2. Follow directions given.

    3. Have an understanding of subject matter.

    4. Avoid distractions.

    5. Show self-discipline by remaining on task.

    6. Be sure to complete the task.

4. ***Model the Skill:***

    A. The teacher will model the skill by telling the students that Mary let herself be interrupted while writing a story for the class when uninvited friends dropped in to ask her some questions.

    B. Students will discuss the situation and suggest a solution.

5. ***Behavioral Rehearsal:***

    A. ***Selection:*** Teacher selects students for role play.

    B. ***Role Plays:*** Use the following situations:

— Student is trying to straighten out the wheel of his bicycle. It is difficult to finish this task by himself. What should he do?

— A student wants to bake a cake but needs the recipe. The mother is not home. What can he/she do?

C. ***Completion:*** After each role play, reinforce correct behavior, identify inappropriate behaviors, and reenact role play with corrections. If there are no corrections, role play is complete.

D. ***Reinforcers:*** Material rewards, verbal praise, nonverbal praise.

E. ***Discussion:*** Students will discuss several solutions to the role play situations.

6. ***Practice:*** Distribute copies of the following worksheet "Completing Assignments," and have students complete it in class and check their work. Also, create a calendar to keep track of assignments completed and have students make individual calendars.

7. ***Independent Use:*** Homework should be completed and returned. Parents will assign a task and insist that the student completes it.

8. ***Continuation:*** Teachers tell students, **"If you use this skill whenever and wherever you need it, you will feel good about yourself and may improve your grades."**

Name _____ Date _____

COMPLETING ASSIGNMENTS

List different things you can do to get your assignments completed on time:

_____

_____

_____

_____

_____

_____

_____

_____

_____

_____

_____

❄❖✳▲❄❖✳▲❄❖✳▲❄❖✳▲❄❖✳▲❄❖✳▲❄❖✳▲❄❖✳▲❄❖✳▲❄❖

Write a poem about completing your work on time:

_____

_____

_____

_____

_____

_____

_____

❄❖✳●❄❖✳✿❄✳✝❄✳▲✳●❄

COMPLETING ASSIGNMENTS Lesson 37

SOCIAL SKILL
Finishing Assignments on Time

Behavioral Objective: The student will finish an assignment within a specified time limit.

Directed Lesson:

1. **Establish the Need:** Completing assignments in a given time will give the student a sense of accomplishment and a useful skill.

2. **Introduction:** The teacher should read the following story:

   "One day in Mr. Smith's class, the students were to complete a mathematics fact test in five minutes. In order to complete all the problems in the time allowed, the students had to begin work when the starting signal was given and work quickly and continuously until they completed the assignment or until time expired. All the students except Terry had the materials necessary to do the work, and began at once, and completed the assignment. Terry had to search for his pencil, worked slowly, looked out the window, and did not complete the assignment in time."

   (1) Why did Terry fail to complete the work? (2) Why did the others complete the work? (3) What grade do you think Terry might receive?

3. **Identify the Skill Components:** (List on the board before class.)

   1. Make sure you know the assignment.
   2. Make sure you have the necessary materials.
   3. Copy down the assignment.
   4. Concentrate to do the assignment.
   5. Skip and return to questions you don't know.
   6. Look over the assignment before handing it in.

4. **Model the Skill:** The teacher will write ten math problems on the board. One student will say go. All ten problems will be done in one minute.

5. **Behavioral Rehearsal:**

   A. **Selection:** Teacher selects three pairs of students to role play.

   B. **Role play:** The teacher will give the class a brief math, art or reading assignment; e.g., "Turn to page 16 in your math book and do problems 1-10 in 15 minutes." Allow the specified time for the assignment to be completed, then grade students' answers.

C. ***Completion:*** After each role play, reinforce correct behavior, identify inappropriate behaviors, and reenact role play with corrections. If there are no corrections, role play is complete.

D. ***Reinforcers:*** Praise and reward students who completed this assignment.

E. ***Discussion:*** Students should discuss the role play and the reasons for the different grades.

6. ***Practice:*** Distribute copies of the activity sheet entitled "Completing Assignment Cartoon" and complete it together in class.

   Give students copies of the activity sheet entitled "Completing Assignment Chart" to do as an individual activity either in class or at home.

7. ***Independent Use:*** Have a family member confirm in writing that the student cleaned his/her room one time during the next week in a specific time limit.

8. ***Continuation:*** Remind students of this skill and the necessity of this skill as related situations arise.

Name _____ Date _____

COMPLETING ASSIGNMENT CARTOON

Skill Steps: When you are given an assignment, you should:

✳▲✳▲✳▲✳▲✳▲✳▲✳▲✳▲✳▲✳▲✳▲✳▲✳▲✳▲✳▲✳▲

A. Make sure you know the assignment.

B. Make sure you have the materials needed to complete the assignment.

C. If you don't understand a question or problem, skip it and return to it later.

D. Look over your work to make sure that it is completed.

✳▲✳▲✳▲✳▲✳▲✳▲✳▲✳▲✳▲✳▲✳▲✳▲✳▲✳▲✳▲✳▲

Directions: Draw a cartoon to illustrate each skill step.

A. Make sure you know the assign-ment.	B. Make sure you have the materials you need.
C. Skip and return to questions you don't know.	D. Look over your work.

✳▲✳▲✳▲✳▲✳▲✳▲✳▲✳▲✳▲✳▲✳▲✳▲✳▲✳▲✳▲✳

Name _____ Date _____

COMPLETING ASSIGNMENT CHART

Skill Steps: When you are given an assignment you should:

    A. Make sure you know the assignment.

    B. Make sure you have the materials needed to complete the assignment.

    C. If you don't understand a question or a problem, skip it and return to it later.

    D. Look over your work to make sure that it is completed.

Activity directions: Keep a record of the assignments that you have completed for a week. If you complete every assignment, give yourself a treat.

Assignment	Mon.	Tues.	Wed.	Thurs.	Fri.
1.					
2.					
3.					
4.					
5.					
6.					
7.					
8.					
9.					
10.					

Lesson 38

SOCIAL SKILL
Working to Complete Assignments

Behavioral Objective: The student will learn to continue working on an assignment until it is completed.

Directed Lesson:

1. ***Establish the Need:*** Tell the students that completing tasks in all areas is very important. If the students do not complete tasks in school, there will probably be a continuation at home. Completing a task gives everyone a feeling of success.

2. ***Introduction:*** Remind the class that there will be a large amount of testing during the school year. Emphasize that many students understand the material, but do not complete the assignment and therefore do not do as well as they should. Give examples of incomplete tests or other unfinished assignments without revealing the identity of the students. (An overhead projector would be helpful.) Remind students that choice is involved, the choice of completing work or giving it up. Remind them of Olympic participants. These people had to overcome many obstacles to do what they wanted to do and to be that good.

3. ***Identify the Skill Components:*** (List on the board before class.)

   1. Listen to directions for doing the assignment.
   2. Think about the assignment.
   3. Read the assignment carefully.
   4. Ask for help by raising your hand if you do not understand.
   5. Notice the time allotment given.
   6. Complete all work.
   7. Check to see if any work has been omitted.
   8. Be sure the classroom guidelines have been followed before handing in your assignment.

4. ***Model the Skill:*** The teacher explains to the class how to complete an assignment. He/she gives a sample assignment and shows how it is to be done.

5. ***Behavioral Rehearsal:***

   A. ***Selection:*** Teacher selects five students to role play.

   B. ***Role Play:*** Use cards that contain activities that the students can role play and complete assignments. Make sure the tasks are simple and short.

C. ***Completion:*** After each role play, reinforce correct behavior, identify inappropriate behaviors, and reenact role play with corrections. If there are no corrections, role play is complete.

D. ***Reinforcers:*** Charts with stars, checks, or smile faces, awards for completing assignments, improved test scores, verbal and nonverbal praise. See the following "The Completed Assignment Award."

E. ***Discussion:*** After the role plays, discuss ways to reinforce using the skill steps to complete assignments.

6. ***Practice:*** Tell the class a story about a set of twins that goes to school. The only way they can be distinguished from each other is by the way they complete or do not complete assignments. Ask the class to take out a piece of paper. Have the students name the twins and write a story about how they were given an assignment or task and how friends were able to tell them apart. Ask them to finish the story by explaining how the twins could become more similar.

7. ***Independent Use:*** Students are to ask family members to assign them a task at home. Have students complete the task, document completion by the person assigning the task, and bring the written document to class.

8. ***Continuation:*** Teachers should remind students how important it is to complete school assignments as well as tasks assigned by adults at home. Being able to complete a job assigned to them shows that they are able to work independently.

Name _____ Date _____

THE COMPLETED ASSIGNMENT

HEAR YE !

HEAR YE!

BE IT KNOWN THAT _____,

AN ILLUSTRIOUS STUDENT, HAS EARNED <u>THE</u>

<u>COMPLETED ASSIGNMENT</u> AWARD AND BADGE.

_____   _____

Date Granted   **Teacher**

☆☆☆☆☆☆☆☆☆☆☆☆☆☆☆☆☆☆☆☆☆☆☆☆

1

Completed

Assignments

PROBLEM SOLVING Lesson 39

SOCIAL SKILL
Listing Problem-Solving Steps

Behavioral Objective: The student will list the steps needed to solve a problem, and apply them in a given situation.

Directed Lesson:

1. ***Establish the Need:*** Discuss with the class the need to be able to solve problems; why we need this skill, and what might happen if one doesn't or is unable to solve problems. (One reason we need this skill of problem solving is to help make right decisions which, for instance, could help avoid confusion.)

2. ***Identify the Skill Components:*** (List on the board.)

   1. Identify the problem.
   2. Think of ways to solve it.
   3. Think about the consequences involved.
   4. Choose the best solution.
   5. Do it.

3. ***Model the Skill:*** Teacher reads the following situation to the class:

   "Jan was leaving school at the end of the day. Her bus was just pulling up to the stop. Suddenly she remembered that she had left her money in her desk at school. She knew her mother would be upset with her. What should she do?"

   Demonstrate to the class the steps in solving Jan's problem. (Use the list on the board.)

4. ***Behavioral Rehearsal:***

   A. ***Selection:*** Divide the class into four groups.

   B. ***Role Play:*** Put the following situations on index cards. Have the students solve the problem. Have one student record the steps followed. After about 10-15 minutes, have each group tell how they solved their problem.

   — Someone borrowed your pencil. Next day, you ask for it, and are told that he/she can't find it. But he/she has a new pencil in hand.

   — A friendly game of baseball is being played in the vacant lot next to Mr. Green's house. You are up to bat. When you hit the ball, it breaks Mr. Green's window. What should you do?

    C. ***Completion:*** After each role play, reinforce correct behavior, identify inappropriate behaviors, and reenact role play with corrections. If there are no corrections, role play is complete.

    D. ***Reinforcers:*** Verbal praise, nonverbal approval (smile, pat, hug).

    E. ***Discussion:*** Discuss role play.

5. ***Practice:*** Distribute copies of the following activity sheet entitled "You Be the Judge" for students to complete in class independently. Discuss the activity with them after they are finished.

6. ***Independent Use:*** Have students write about a problem they had to solve in school, at home, or with friends. Students can share their writings on Friday.

7. ***Continuation:*** Teachers should continue to encourage students to think of problem-solving alternatives as related situations arise.

CHILDREN'S LITERATURE

Moss, Thylias. *I Want to Be.* Illustrated by Jerry Pinkney. New York: Dial Books, 1993.

Name _____ Date _____

YOU BE THE JUDGE !

UNSCRAMBLE THE FOLLOWING WORDS:

u n s t i l o o _____

p m r o e l b _____

h n k i t _____

s o e e q u c n n s c _____

e s c h o o _____

WRITE SOLUTIONS TO THE FOLLOWING PROBLEMS. REMEMBER THE STEPS.

#1 Your best friend asked someone you don't like to come to a pajama party. Will you go or stay home?

#2 Your school is having an assembly program tomorrow and YOU are giving the opening speech. Last night your cold got worse and you can hardly talk. What will you do, give the speech anyway or talk it over with the teacher?

#3 You are the teacher and have been asked to select three students who scored above average on their math test to be in a contest. Actually, four students fit the criteria. How will you select the three?

LIST THE STEPS YOU HAVE LEARNED FOR SOLVING A PROBLEM.

1 .
2 .
3 .
4 .
5 .

SOCIAL SKILL
Making a Decision

Behavioral Objective: The student will make a decision when given a situation.

Directed Lesson:

1. ***Establish the Need:*** Review with the students the fact that in our daily lives we are faced with making decisions. Therefore, it is important that we know how decisions are made. Ask what might happen if we didn't know how to make a decision. (Sample responses: confusion, nothing will get solved, may be harmful to us, etc.)

2. ***Identify the Skill Components:*** (List on the board.)

    1. Think about the problem.
    2. Think about the choices.
    3. Think about the advantages/consequences.
    4. Choose the best solution.
    5. Make a decision.

3. ***Model the Skill:*** Teacher reads the following situation to the class:

    "Johnny had been looking forward to this weekend. He would be going to Sea World with his sister, brother, and parents. That Friday after school, Johnny's best friend, Al, asked him if he could do a favor for him this weekend. Al wanted Johnny to do his paper route for him because he had a doctor's appointment. If he missed a day not doing the route, he would get fired."

    What should Johnny do? Teacher shows class how a decision should be made by going through the steps.

4. ***Behavioral Rehearsal:***

    A. ***Selection:*** Have students volunteer to role play the following situations, demonstrating the process of decision making.

    B. ***Role Play:***

    1. ***Situation:*** A decision must be made to eat breakfast and be late for school or not to eat and be on time.

    2. ***Situation:*** To do homework and practice or not do homework and go outside to play.

3. ***Situation:*** Go with my friend to the store or go straight home like my parents would want me to do.

C. ***Completion:*** After each role play, reinforce correct behavior, identify inappropriate behaviors, and reenact role play with corrections. If there are no corrections, role play is complete.

D. ***Reinforcers:*** Verbal praise, nonverbal approval, group reinforcement.

E. ***Discussion:*** Discuss role plays.

5. ***Practice:*** Distribute copies of the following activity sheet, entitled "Decisions', Decissions.'" and complete it with the class.

6. ***Independent Use:*** Have students solve the problem of a student who was walking home from school and was approached by a man giving away toys. He asks you to come to his house. What do you do?

7. ***Continuation:*** Teachers should point out the continuing need for each person to make decisions in every aspect of his/her life.

Name _____   Date _____

DECISIONS, DECISIONS !

Susan must make a decision about a problem she is having. Help her by tracing the path she should take in order to solve it.

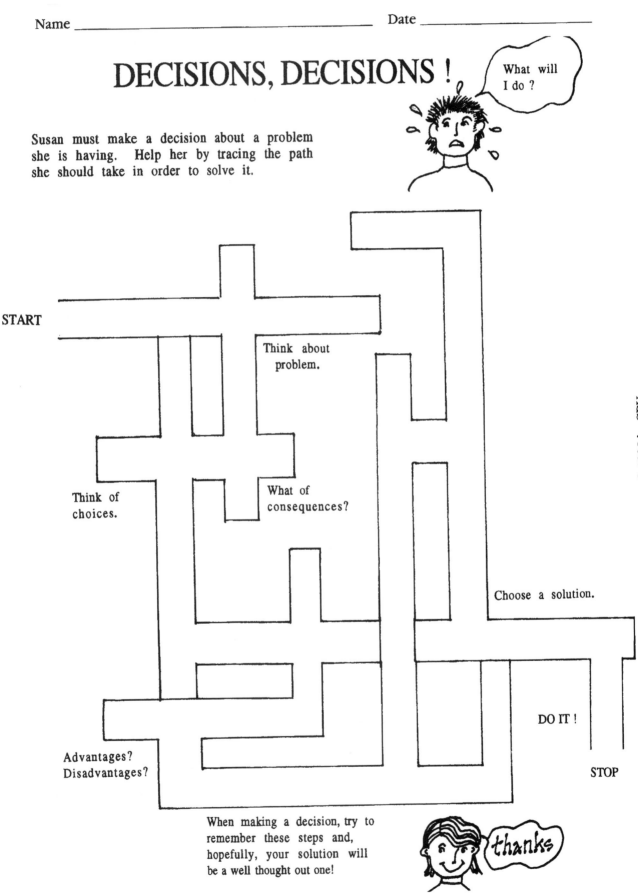

What will I do ?

START

Think about problem.

Think of choices.

What of consequences?

Choose a solution.

DO IT !

STOP

Advantages?
Disadvantages?

When making a decision, try to remember these steps and, hopefully, your solution will be a well thought out one!

thanks

PROBLEM SOLVING

Lesson 41

SOCIAL SKILL
Reviewing Problem-Solving Choices

Behavioral Objective: The student will review various choices and predetermined consequences before making a decision.

Directed Lesson:

1. **Establish the Need:** This skill is necessary for social and academic success now and in the future.

2. **Introduction:** Teacher reads the following situation to the class:

   "One evening, Sam Goodbody had been invited to go the movies with one of his friends. Sam had at least forty minutes of homework to do. He had to leave for the movie in ten minutes. What should he do?"

   Teacher will list on the board the choices and consequences that the class suggests Sam should consider. Then ask several students what decision they would make if they were Sam.

3. **Identify the Skill Components:** (List on the board before class.)

   1. Think about your choices.
   2. List all of your choices.
   3. Think about and list a consequence for each choice.
   4. Decide if the consequence fits each choice.
   5. Review all of your information and make a decision.

4. **Model the Skill:** Teacher will choose a questionable situation and list choices and consequences necessary to solve the problem and make a decision based on the information.

5. **Behavioral Rehearsal:**

   A. **Selection:** Teacher selects six students to role play.

   B. **Role Play:** Use the following activity sheet, entitled "The Interview," as a guide. Five students will make up a problem and then decide how a decision was reached about the student they interviewed.

   C. **Completion:** After each role play, reinforce correct behavior, identify inappropriate behaviors, and reenact role play with corrections. If there are no corrections, role play is complete.

   D. **Reinforcers:** Verbal praise, self-praise, group reinforcement.

    E. ***Discussion:*** Students will discuss possible ways of reaching a decision based on information about positive and negative consequences.

6. ***Practice:*** Distribute copies of the activity sheet entitled "The Interview" and do it together in class.

7. ***Independent Use:*** Ask students to complete the "Transfer Activity" sheet at home, have it signed by a parent, and return it to school within the next week.

8. ***Continuation:*** Teachers should point out the need for considering alternative solutions to problems in all areas of life.

Name _____ Date _____

THE INTERVIEW

Directions: Five of you will choose a student in your classroom to interview. You will interview him/her, then he/she will interview all five of you.

Name of person being interviewed: _____

State the problem or situation:

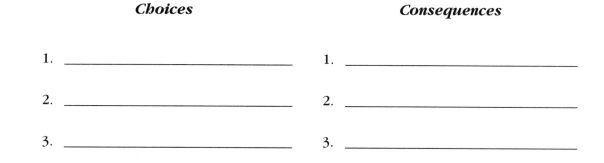

Choices	*Consequences*
1. _____	1. _____
2. _____	2. _____
3. _____	3. _____

What was the decision?

Do you think the group made a wise decision? Why or why not?

Name _____ Date _____

TRANSFER ACTIVITY

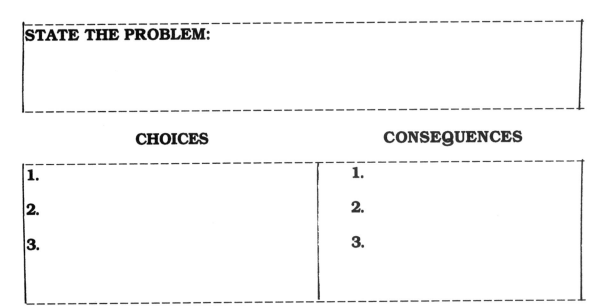

Problem-Solving/Decision-Making Skill Steps

1. List choices.
2. List consequences.
3. Make your decision.

DIRECTIONS: Complete this activity sheet by describing a problem that came up at your home and show how you decided to solve it.

STATE THE PROBLEM:

CHOICES	CONSEQUENCES
1.	1.
2.	2.
3.	3.

What did you decide to do? How did it work out?

PROBLEM SOLVING

SOCIAL SKILL
Managing Conflict

Behavioral Objective: The students will use decision-making skills in the process of daily conflicts and situations.

Directed Lesson:

1. ***Establish the Need:*** The importance of conflict management is found in the realities of everyday living. Hardly any person can say that they are not faced with conflicts and pressures that they must deal with. Students need to know how to balance conflicting situations so that they can effectively control their emotions and not experience extreme problems which are difficult to solve, so that they are doing either nothing about the situation or are permanently terminating the situation, by death such as committing suicide.

2. ***Introduction:*** The terms conflict and management need to be defined. Also, review the decision-making skills from the previous lesson (if completed).

    1. A conflict is a situation where you have two or more issues or problems to deal with, all of which need to be resolved in time. There is a mental struggle involved where you have opposing needs, wishes and drives, all having the same weighted value.

    2. Management is the way you control your life and situations by using a clear, well-thought-out decision-making process.

3. ***Identify the Skill Components:*** (List on board before class.)

    1. List your choices.

    2. List your consequences.

    3. Decide on the choice that has the least negative consequence.

    4. Ask yourself if that choice is fair and conscientious.

4. ***Model the Skill:*** Read the following situation and discuss the questions that follow.

    "James is just getting home from track practice at his high school. He has two homework assignments to complete, one for math and one for reading. They both will take him an hour or so to finish and they both have to be completed for class tomorrow. However James has time for only one of them since he and his parents have to attend a funeral service for a family member. It will be late by the time he gets home and he has to be up at 6:30 the next morning to catch the bus."

    1. Should James do the math assignment (40 problems), or the reading assignment (32 pages)?

137

2. When is he going to find the time to finish the other assignment?

3. What may be the consequence of not completing one or the other assignment?

4. If James does some work after he comes home that night, what consequences might arise?

5. ***Behavioral Rehearsal:***

   A. ***Selection:*** Teacher selects three pairs of students to role play.

   B. ***Role Play:*** Read to the students these situations where a conflict exists. Follow the skill steps for each one by listing them on the board.

   — Robert is in the band and plays the trumpet. He has to practice every day after school with the band leader. However, tonight he also has a science report to finish which he hasn't even started. What should he do?

   — Jean sees Terry stealing a bracelet from another friend's desk. Jean is confused because she likes the other girl whose bracelet is stolen although she and Terry are best of friends. What should she do?

   — Darnelle has a stack of chores to finish. His friends come over and want him to practice frisbee-throwing for the contest tomorrow in which the first prize is $25.00. He knows he could use the money for his mother's upcoming birthday present. What should he do?

   C. ***Completion:*** After each role play, reinforce correct behavior, identify inappropriate behaviors, and reenact role play with corrections. If there are no corrections, role play is complete.

   D. ***Reinforcers:*** Verbal praise, self-praise, group reinforcement.

   E. ***Discussion:*** Discuss by evaluating the student's response and how well the skill steps were used.

6. ***Practice:*** To practice this skill, have students complete the following activity sheet entitled "Malcolm's Conflict."

7. ***Independent Use:*** Have students tell about a conflict they resolved or did not resolve during the week. Distribute the activity sheet "Decision Time." Have students select a conflict for this activity, complete the activity sheet at home, and bring it to class a week following the assignment for discussion.

8. ***Continuation:*** Teacher should point out the need for decision-making skills in managing conflicts in life, as related situations arise.

Name _____ Date _____

MALCOLM'S CONFLICT

* *

Skill Steps:

1. List your choices.

2. List your consequences.

3. Decide on the choice that has the least consequences.

4. Ask yourself if that choice is also fair and conscientious.

* *

Now that we have discussed the ways by which conflicts can be resolved, you are going to do the same with the following situation. Read the conflict, then follow the skill steps to resolve it. Finally, make an illustration that depicts how you resolved it. Use the back page of this worksheet.

"Malcolm is an excellent dancer and singer. He is also talented in basketball and running. Malcolm decides to join the choir instead of a sports team because that is what his parents feel is best. His other friends say that he is involved in 'girls' activities and tease him enough that he decides to quit the choir, and considers a sports team. However, he is upset with the people who he thought were his friends. Should he go back to the choir which was his first desire, or remain with the sports team which he also enjoys?"

Name _____ Date _____

DECISION TIME

The conflict is as follows: or make box for describing a conflict.

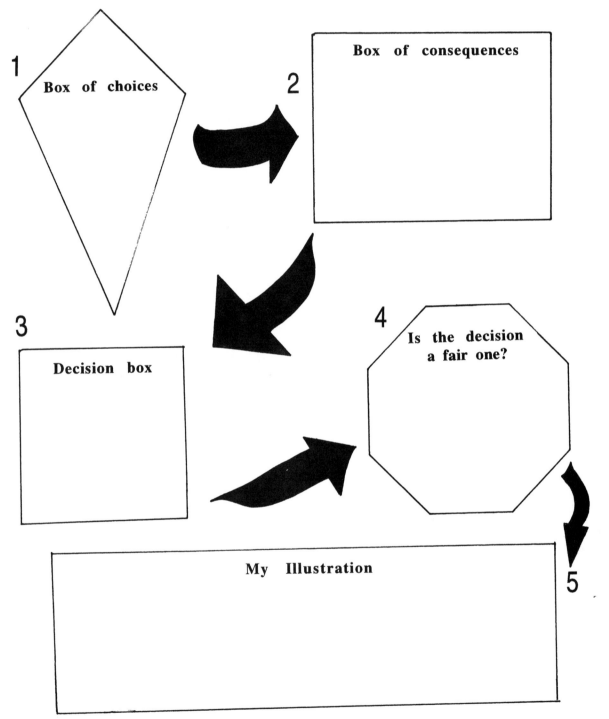

1 Box of choices

2 Box of consequences

3 Decision box

4 Is the decision a fair one?

5

My Illustration

PROBLEM SOLVING

SOCIAL SKILL
Applying a Method to Solve Problems

Behavioral Objective: The student will be able to state and to apply a method for solving problems.

Directed Lesson:

1. **Establish the Need:** Problems can be more readily solved if they are approached in a step-by-step method. If there is not a method for solving the problem, the solution may never come, or come with much difficulty.

2. **Introduction:** Teacher reads:

    "What do my burnt brownies have in common with Fred's little brother??? We both have problems that occur over and over again, and we both need a way to SOLVE our problems!! Suppose every time I make brownies they turn out too dry and hard, and every time Fred tries to play with his little brother, they end up fighting and Fred gets the blame! Sounds like a problem for Sherlock Hound, expert and professional PROBLEM SOLVER!

    Have students use the following dog puppet "Sherlock Hound" to describe the super sleuth's methodology, also known as "use skill components for problem solving."

3. **Identify the Skill Components:** (List on board before class.)

    1. State the problem.
    2. List possible causes of problem.
    3. Brainstorm many different solutions.
    4. Decide on the best solutions.
    5. Try the solution.
    6. Evaluate the solution.
    7. Redesign the solution if necessary.

4. **Model the Skill:** The teacher uses the example of burnt brownies to show how she/he would solve the problem using the steps; i.e., use a different recipe, test the temperature of the oven, etc.

5. **Behavioral Rehearsal:**

    A. **Selection:** Include each student in role plays. Class will divide into groups of six, each group having one student designated as secretary.

B. ***Role Play:*** Each student writes a problem on a piece of paper without giving his/her name. Each group chooses a problem from the "hat," and applies the method outlined to the problem. Class observes each group noting whether the steps are carefully followed. The secretary writes the problem, the possible cause(s), and the possible solution(s) on the board. The class votes on the best solution after discussing the benefits of each solution.

C. ***Completion:*** After each role play, reinforce correct behavior, identify inappropriate behaviors, and reenact role play with corrections. If there are no corrections, role play is complete.

D. ***Reinforcers:*** Verbal praise for the correct method and a good solution.

E. ***Discussion:*** The students discuss the various solutions and why they did or did not succeed in solving the problem.

6. ***Practice:*** Teacher uses word problems from the math book and has students tell and apply a method for solving each one.

7. ***Independent Use:*** Each student must complete a homework assignment in which he/she identifies a problem of his/her own, and applies the skill steps to it. A week is given to carry out the assignment. The evaluation must offer hypotheses on why the solution worked or failed to work.

8. ***Continuation:*** As related situations arise, teachers should remind students that it is usually best to apply a step-by-step method in solving problems.

Name _____ Date _____

SHERLOCK HOUND

Color Sherlock Hound.
Make his badge look
interesting too!

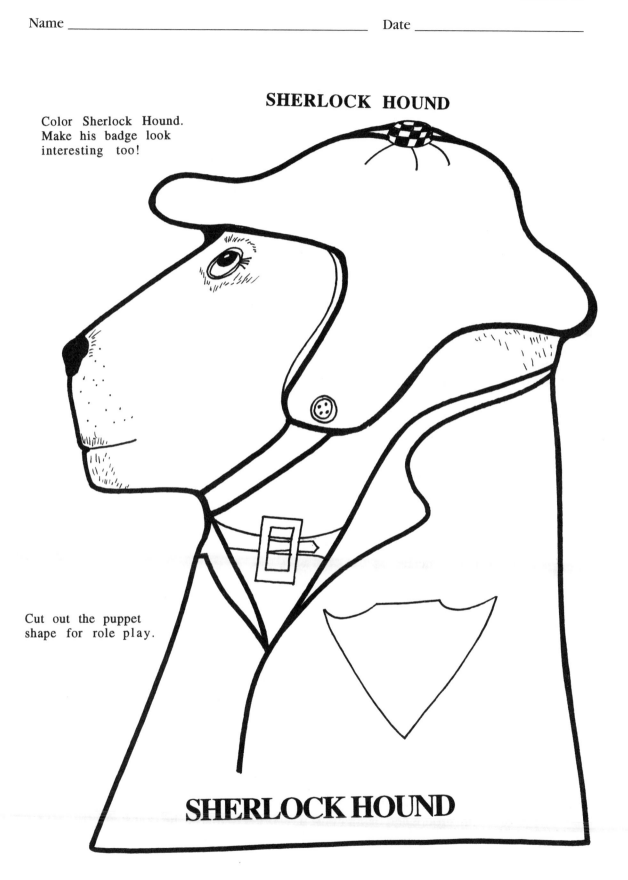

Cut out the puppet
shape for role play.

SHERLOCK HOUND

SOCIAL SKILL
Using a Plan to Solve Problems

Behavioral Objective: The student will be able to use a definite plan to solve problems.

Directed Lesson:

1. ***Establish the Need:*** Discuss with the class the importance of this skill. Stress that problems in the classroom, school, and home could be solved more easily with a definite plan.

2. ***Introduction:*** Write the words *alternatives* and *consequences* on the board. Pass file cards to students that contain simulated problems. A recorder should write the responses elicited by the class on the board. Ask the students to give a reason for having a plan to solve these problems.

3. ***Identify the Skill Components:*** (List on board before class.)

   1. Stop and think before speaking.
   2. Decide what you think the problem is.
   3. List different ways the problem can be solved.
   4. Make a choice.
   5. Try using the choice you made.
   6. Evaluate the choice.

4. ***Model the Skill:*** The teacher models solving a problem following the skill steps. *Problem:* A parent wants to come in for a conference with the teacher this afternoon, but the teacher has another appointment.

5. ***Behavioral Rehearsal:***

   A. ***Selection:*** One student will role play a situation. Then the class will be divided into groups.

   B. ***Role Play:*** A student role plays coming to school without his homework. The student insists that he has lost the homework; however, the teacher doesn't believe him. He receives an "F" for the assignment and a treat that was scheduled previously is taken away from him. Using the skill steps above, determine what behavioral options this student has.

   The next activity is for the class to write some problems of their own. Divide the students into groups and let them use a recorder to follow the skill steps. Using the recorded results, let each group present their data to the class.

    C. ***Completion:*** After each role play, reinforce correct behavior, identify inappropriate behaviors, and reenact role play with corrections. If there are no corrections, role play is complete.

    D. ***Reinforcers:*** Use verbal praise to reinforce correct behavior, and correct inappropriate behavior. Badges are other reinforcement that can be used.

    E. ***Discussion:*** Permit the class to agree or disagree with the decisions of the groups from the role play activity.

6. ***Practice:*** Distribute copies of the following activity sheet, "My Plan," and have students complete it in class. Each student is to select a problem then devise his/her own plan for solving the problem.

7. ***Independent Use:*** Establish a school-wide student organization to help solve school problems.

8. ***Continuation:*** Teachers should remind students that most problems can be solved more easily when we have a plan to solve them.

Name _____ Date _____

MY PLAN

Directions: Describe a problem in the space below, then write your plan for solving the problem. List each step in your plan showing how to solve the problem.

The problem: _____

_____

_____

_____

My problem-solving plan:

1. _____

Determine if this problem can be solved *today* or do you need time to work on the solution? If you need time, determine how much time is needed and work that into your plan.

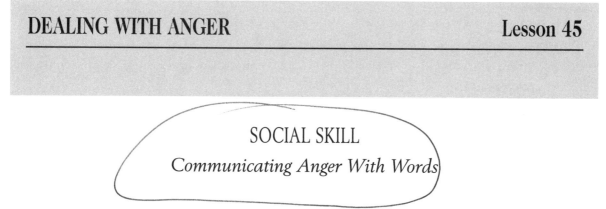

SOCIAL SKILL
Communicating Anger With Words

Behavioral Objective: When angry with a peer, the student will express anger with nonaggressive words rather than physical actions or aggressive words.

Directed Lesson:

1. ***Establish the Need:*** Teacher will discuss that expressing anger with nonaggressive words should bring about a faster and a more positive solution to the problem. Aggressive words or physical actions can only result in prolonging the problem or making it worse.

2. ***Introduction:*** Teacher will read the following story to the students:

   > **"John just got a Christmas present from Uncle Bob. John likes his uncle very much and was happy with the fire engine toy, which he could steer by use of remote control. The day after Christmas, he took the fire engine to his friend, Mike, and both played with it. It was fun. John's mother called John and requested that he join her and his sister for lunch. John left the fire engine with Mike, who continued to play with it, but he did not know how to steer it, and then in annoyance, kicked it. The toy was damaged. One of the rear wheels broke loose.**

   > **"Needless to say, when John returned after lunch and saw what had happened, he was very angry. Why should Mike have done what he did? John's first reaction was to hit Mike. But on second thought, John realized that hitting Mike would not repair the fire engine. However, John wanted Mike to know he was very angry, and told him so. John's proper behavior made Mike even aware that he should not have done what he did, and he apologized. Mike repaired the damage with the help of his father."**

   1. Feedback: Students will give positive comments on the way John handled this situation.
   2. Teacher will discuss the rewards gained when one performs the skill.
   3. Teacher and students will discuss behaviors needed to perform this skill.
   4. Teacher and students will discuss the consequence for performing and not performing this skill.

3. ***Identify the Skill Components:*** (List on board.)

   1. Count to ten.
   2. Ask yourself why you are angry.
   3. Think about what you should do.

4. Say "I'm upset, let's discuss this further."

5. Tell the other student why you are angry, stating what he/she has done and how it affects you.

4. ***Model the Skill:*** Teacher models the skill by reading a story that shows how to express anger with nonaggressive words.

5. ***Behavioral Rehearsal:***

A. ***Selection:*** Students volunteer to role play.

B. ***Role Play:*** The teacher will give the students role-play situations in which they pretend to be angry at a student and have to demonstrate the appropriate behavior.

— One student steals another student's lunch money.

— One student cuts in front of another.

— One student trips another.

C. ***Completion:*** After each role play, reinforce correct behavior, identify inappropriate behaviors, and reenact role play with corrections. If there are no corrections, role play is complete.

D. ***Reinforcers:*** Material rewards, verbal praise, nonverbal expression of approval (smile, pat, hug), group reinforcement.

E. ***Discussion:*** Students give feedback on how they felt about the role plays, whether they needed to suggest changes, and what they learned.

6. ***Practice:*** Distribute copies of the following activity sheet "Poster Art" and have students do it in class.

7. ***Independent Usage:*** Have family members record and report back to school when the student demonstrates the learned behavior. Student should be rewarded.

8. ***Continuation:*** Teachers should continue pointing out that expressing one's anger in nonaggressive words almost always helps to solve a problem more quickly and positively.

CHILDREN'S LITERATURE

Lattimore, Deborah Norse. *Why There Is No Arguing in Heaven, a Mayan Myth.* NY: Harper & Row, 1989.

Name _____ Date _____

POSTER ART

Directions: We are surrounded by poster art and by slogans. Look through a variety of magazines and newspapers for ideas. Then, put your own ideas to work to design an anti-anger poster in the space below.

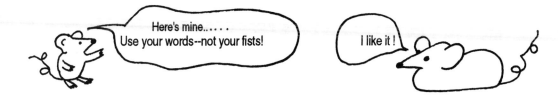

DEALING WITH ANGER

SOCIAL SKILL
Controlling One's Anger

Behavioral Objective: When angry with a peer, the student will walk away or use some other constructive means to avoid hitting or showing temperament.

Directed Lesson:

1. **Establish the Need:** Discuss how controlling one's anger can bring about successful academic and social benefits.

2. **Introduction:** The teacher will tell the following situation:

   "When students in Mr. Smith's class got in line for a drink of water, two students, Terry and Joe, would always cause a commotion. One of them would push or hit the other who then would push; or hit back; thus they would cause a disturbance. Mr. Smith warned them that it was dangerous to push someone and that hitting was not permitted. They were told to report to him if someone pushed or hit them. But, Terry and Joe continued the practice. What do you think will happen next?"

   1. Teacher will discuss what the student should do when he/she becomes angry at another person. Teacher will tell the student that instead of hitting when you become angry, just walk away from the person. Another alternative is to tell an adult about what it is that is making you angry.

   2. Teacher will discuss the consequences for appropriate and inappropriate behaviors. Teacher may wish to have comments from students when setting up consequences.

3. **Identify the Skill Components:** (List on board.)

   1. Control your emotions.

   2. Walk away from the person with whom you are angry.

   3. Go to an adult and tell him/her what made you angry.

4. **Model the Skill:** The teacher can demonstrate various situations in which he/she takes the role of dealing with an angry student.

5. **Behavioral Rehearsal:**

   A. **Selection:** Students volunteer to role play.

   B. **Role Play:** Teachers will give students situations which they can role play and practice to learn the appropriate way of how to handle this skill.

— Student throws another student's homework away.

— Student trips someone.

C. ***Completion:*** After each role play, reinforce correct behavior, identify inappropriate behaviors, and reenact role play with corrections. If there are no corrections, role play is complete.

D. ***Reinforcers:*** Material rewards, verbal praise, nonverbal expression of approval (smile, pat, hug), group reinforcement. The teacher verbally praises those who controlled their anger and walked away. Teacher can also set up a contingency contract with certain students.

E. ***Discussion:*** Let students discuss how they felt about the way the role plays were presented.

6. ***Practice:*** Distribute copies of the following activity sheet entitled "What Should You Do?" and complete it in class.

7. ***Independent Use:*** Encourage students to transfer what they have learned when dealing with situations on the playground or lunchroom. Have them write an example situation at home and have them share it with the class one week from today.

8. ***Continuation:*** Teachers should continue pointing out the need for controlling one's anger as related situations arise.

CHILDREN'S LITERATURE

Sherlock, Philip. *Anansi the Spider Man,* Jamaican Folk Tales. Illustrated by Marcia Brown, NY: Thomas Y. Crowell, 1954.

This is one of many offerings about Anansi the trickster who wins some and loses some.

Name _____ Date _____

WHAT SHOULD YOU DO?

Directions: Choose the best answer to each question. Draw a CIRCLE around your answer.

1. You are walking down the hall and another student trips you. What should you do?

   a. hit the person

   b. chase the person

   c. tell the teacher

   d. yell at the person

2. You are standing in line to go to lunch. Another student cuts in front of you in line. What should you do?

   a. push the person out of line

   b. hit the person

   c. yell at the person— Hope

   d. ignore the person— Justin

3. You are sitting at your desk. You see another student throw someone's homework away. What should you do?

   a. yell at the person

   b. tell the person you saw him/her

   c. tell the teacher — all

   d. jump up and hit the person

4. You are doing some work at your desk. Another student accuses you of stealing his/her crayons. You know you are innocent. What should you do?

   a. call the person a name

   b. hit the person

   c. tell the person how you feel

   d. yell at the person

5. You are taking a test. Another student starts to copy from your paper. What should you do?

   a. tell him/her to stop

   b. yell at the person

   c. push him/her away

   d. grab the paper and tear it up

6. You wear glasses. Another student calls you names and teases you about it. What should you do?

   a. ignore the person

   b. hit him/her

   c. yell at the person

   d. chase him/her

7. You are eating lunch. Someone knocks your food on the floor. What should you do?

    a. knock his/her food on the floor

    b. hit the person

    c. tell the lunch aide what happened

    d. yell at him/her

8. You are playing a game. Another student keeps yelling out the names of the persons who are playing with you. What should you do?

    a. stop the game

    b. hit the person

    c. yell at the person

    d. tell the teacher

9. You are playing on the playground. Another student keeps hitting you and running away. What should you do?

    a. chase the person

    b. hit the person

    c. tell the playground supervisor

    d. yell at the person

When finished, discuss the possible solutions with classmates and teacher. Keep an open mind. Think about it. You may even decide to change an answer.

Hmmm! Maybe that is a better way to handle this!

DEALING WITH ANGER

SOCIAL SKILL
Using Self-Control Steps

Behavioral Objective: The students will control their anger by using skills steps to keep self-control.

Directed Lesson:

1. ***Establish the Need:*** The skill of self-control is necessary to control anger, to prevent destructive behavior, and to reinforce and resolve conflicts in a nonviolent way.

2. ***Introduction:*** The teacher should read the following situation:

   "On Wednesday morning, Sherdina was already sitting at her desk when Jane walked down the aisle toward her seat. Sherdina casually stuck out her foot and tripped Jane. Jane fell and bloodied her nose. Jane became furious, and started angrily toward Sherdina. What skill steps should Jane use to deal with her anger?"

3. ***Identify the Skill Components:*** (List on board before class.)

   1. Stop and try to relax.
   2. Breathe deeply.
   3. State why you are angry.
   4. Walk away when appropriate.

4. ***Model the Skill:*** Teacher will role play situations in which he/she can use skill steps to demonstrate how to deal with anger.

5. ***Behavioral Rehearsal:***

   A. ***Selection:*** Teacher selects students for role play.

   B. ***Role Play:*** Students role play the following situations.

   — Someone takes your seat when you get up to throw something away in the lunchroom garbage can.

   — You are waiting in line to get a drink and someone lets another person in line before you.

   — You are drawing a picture and someone bumps your desk which causes you to draw a crooked line.

   C. ***Completion:*** After each role play, reinforce correct behavior, identify inappropriate behaviors, and reenact role play with corrections. If there are no corrections, role play is complete.

154

    D. ***Reinforcers:*** Material rewards, verbal praise, group reinforcement.

    E. ***Discussion:*** Students will discuss how you should deal with anger in acceptable ways.

6. ***Practice:*** Distribute copies of the following activity sheet entitled "Sorting Out Anger" to do together in class.

7. ***Independent Use:*** Students will question their parents about when they got angry and how they resolved the situation and report to class their discussions.

8. ***Continuation:*** Teachers should continue pointing out the need for this skill as related situations arise.

Name _____ Date _____

SORTING OUT ANGER

DIRECTIONS:
Circle only the words that resolve anger according to the skill steps.   Then find
these words in the word search.   Words can be in any direction.

COUNT	TRIP	TELL	SWEAR
STOP	RELAXATION	DISCUSS	FIGHT
ANGRY	CHOICES	ACT	KICK
PUNCH	WALK	SCREAM	SCRATCH
RESOLVE	BREATHE	CONTROL	APPROPRIATE

```
T   B   A   R   K   E   A   X   T   I   H   P   A

R   Y   L   F   W   T   B   G   J   C   Z   O   K

E   O   V   U   M   A   L   Z   B   O   Q   E   W

L   E   C   H   C   I   C   E   S   N   I   E   Z

A   V   L   N   R   R   U   T   G   T   T   H   E

X   P   O   T   S   P   B   I   Y   R   C   T   I

A   R   J   U   B   O   H   Y   N   O   K   A   J

T   U   W   M   U   R   E   S   O   L   V   E   Q

I   S   N   Z   R   P   P   Q   A   E   D   R   O

O   L   L   E   T   P   T   W   Y   O   A   B   V

N   W   O   A   J   A   R   M   G   L   H   Y   I

C   O   U   N   T   I   S   S   U   C   S   I   D
```

DEALING WITH ANGER

Lesson 48

SOCIAL SKILL
Using Self-Control Steps

Behavioral Objective: The student will control his/her anger by using skill steps to keep self-control.

Directed Lesson:

1. **Establish the Need:** The skill of self-control is necessary to control anger, to prevent destructive behavior and to reinforce and resolve conflicts in a nonviolent way.

2. **Introduction:** The teacher should read the following situation:

   "John was sitting quietly in his homeroom when Terry came into the room and started yelling at him. John did not know why Terry was yelling and asked, 'Why are you yelling at me?' Terry said it was because someone told him John had called him a name. John said he had not called anyone names and that the other person was not telling the truth. The teacher said John was not guilty and that perhaps the friend had just told a story to make Terry act out."

   With this teacher's decision, how should John and Terry react?

3. **Identify the Skill Components:** (List on board before class.)

   1. Stop and try to relax.
   2. Breathe deeply.
   3. State why you are angry.
   4. Walk away when appropriate.
   5. Try to resolve the situation.

4. **Model the Skill:** Teacher will role play situations in which he/she can use skill steps to demonstrate how to deal with anger.

5. **Behavioral Rehearsal:**

   A. **Selection:** The teacher will select four students for each role play to model the behavior.

   B. **Role Play:** Students role play the following situations.

   — **"I hate you! You're not my friend any more."**

   — **"You broke my favorite record, so I'm going to break yours."**

   — **"You ruined my favorite sweater, and you didn't even ask to borrow it."**

   — **The angry father said, "Why didn't you cut the grass this morning?"**

157

    C. ***Completion:*** After each role play, reinforce correct behavior, identify inappropriate behaviors, and reenact role play with corrections. If there are no corrections, role play is complete.

    D. ***Reinforcers:*** Material rewards, verbal praise, group reinforcement.

    E. ***Discussion:*** Students discuss the proper way of handling another person's anger and the necessity of having the feelings of both sides of a conflict explained.

6. ***Practice:*** Distribute copies of the following activity sheet entitled "Resolving Anger" and have students complete it together in class.

7. ***Independent Use:*** Give each student a copy of the activity sheet entitled "A Conflict Taken From History." Each student will write a paragraph describing how an angry conflict was resolved.

8. ***Continuation:*** Teachers should continue pointing out the need for controlling anger as related situations arise.

CHILDREN'S LITERATURE

Fritz, Jean. *Shh! We're Writing the Constitution.* NY: Putnam. 1987.

A good short story that shows the necessity for compromise and give-and-take when working with others.

Name _____ Date _____

RESOLVING ANGER

Write an essay describing a situation where someone was angry with you. How was it resolved?

_____

_____

_____

_____

_____

_____

_____

_____

_____

_____

_____

_____

_____

Beside the rainbow, write a few words or phrases that helped you resolve your situation, and write one solution that can be used in any situation. Color the rainbow.

_____

_____

_____

_____

_____

Name _____ Date _____

A CONFLICT TAKEN FROM HISTORY

Write a paragraph describing a conflict that occurred in history that you are currently studying, which tells how the conflict situation was resolved. Draw an illustration that depicts the situation in a picture or cartoon form.

_____

_____

_____

_____

_____

_____

_____

_____

_____

_____

_____

SOCIAL SKILL
Recognizing Words That Spark Anger

Behavioral Objective: The student will identify words that trigger anger and be able to describe self as having a "short" or "long" fuse based on self-appraisal.

Directed Lesson:

1. **Establish the Need:** If students recognize words that trigger their own anger, they might learn to ignore them. Students need also to be aware that certain words cause other people to become angry. They should avoid using these words because they often lead to confrontation or anger.

2. **Introduction:** Ask students how many of them know a word or name that will make their brother or sister "lose it" (cry, fight, or yell)? How many of them have a brother or sister who can make the student himself/herself "lose it" by calling a special name or saying a particular word?

3. **Identify the Skill Components:** (List on board before class.)

    1. Recognize what "trigger words" are.
    2. Recognize which "trigger words" are most powerful for you.
    3. Recognize which "trigger words" are most powerful for others.
    4. Decide whether you have a "long fuse" or a "short fuse."
    5. Ignore these trigger words when you hear them.
    6. Avoid using any trigger words with others.

4. **Model the Skill:** Teacher models a scene where a student calls another student a name that serves as a "trigger word." Discuss whether the student has a long or a short fuse and how the situation should be handled and resolved.

5. **Behavioral Rehearsal:**

    A. **Selection:** All students will take part in Part I of the role play. The teacher will select pairs of students for Part II of the role play.

    B. **Role Play:** Part I: Ask students to recall words that spark fights and arguments. List them on the board and have the class vote on the words that are most aggressive. Discuss why they think these words are so powerful. Speculate with students if they think that the people using these words realize that they are aggressive. Develop the idea of a "trigger," showing students that not only words but other metaphors such as "pushing a button" can trigger too. Ask for other possible metaphors that convey the idea of an AUTOMATIC response. Make sure the students understand that EVERYONE

161

IS SENSITIVE to some things and that this vulnerability varies from person to person and from period to period in one's life. Encourage students to think about how quickly they react to the "trigger words," and admonish students to avoid the use of such metaphors.

Part II: One student will use a "trigger word," while the other will react by using some of the skill steps.

C. ***Completion:*** After each role play, reinforce correct behavior, identify inappropriate behaviors, and reenact role play with corrections. If there are no corrections, role play is complete.

D. ***Reinforcers:*** Verbal and nonverbal praise.

E. ***Discussion:*** Discuss how the sensitivity of students can give power to others when making comments. Ask students for the best way to handle "trigger words" so that the power of the words fades.

6. ***Practice:*** Distribute copies of the following activity sheet entitled "Trigger Words and Personal Identity." Review that "trigger words" have power because of personal sensitivities. Select areas of sensitivity, such as social status, and determine what words might arouse anger. Write these words outside the figure. Use various areas of sensitivity.

7. ***Independent Use:*** Create a character, a hero/heroine, who understands the power of "trigger words" and has defenses against such tactics. For example:

HUMOROUS HELEN who finds the funny side to put-downs <u>and</u> turns insults into jokes!

RUBBERSKIN RALPH so impervious that insults just bounce right off, who ruins all the fun for the playground bullies . . . they <u>can't</u> get him to react!

COOL MAN LUKE . . . so cool, so calm, so laid-back that fiery words lose their sting when he smiles and says, "Sounds like you have the problem, not me!"

Students may design posters with their heroes/heroines showing off their particular DEFENSE PROWESS.

This activity is aimed at helping students broaden their repertoire of strategies when faced with "trigger words." It also intends to give nonviolent behavior dignity, value and prestige.

8. ***Continuation:*** Teachers should remind students that each of us is sensitive to certain words. We should know the words that anger us and control our reactions to them.

Name _____ Date _____

TRIGGER WORDS AND PERSONAL IDENTITY

Select an area of sensitivity that might arouse anger. Then, think of five "trigger words" and write them in the space provided.

TRIGGER WORDS FOR AREA OF SENSITIVITY:_____

1.
2.
3.
4.
5.

SOCIAL SKILL
Recognizing Another's Anger

Behavioral Objective: Student will learn to recognize and understand another's anger.

Directed Lesson:

1. ***Establish the Need:*** Teacher will stress the importance of not becoming angry when another party is angry. Explain what happens when two people become angry. Show how social behavior can improve when one of the two persons can remain calm. Remind students of the steps used in maintaining self-control. Remind them that this too is self-control. It is also very important to understand that others can become angry and that we must accept this emotion, remain calm, and deal with it.

2. ***Introduction:*** The teacher can refer to popular T.V. shows that show violence. Discuss with the class why there is so much shooting. What could be done to reduce or prevent the violence? How can understanding the emotion of anger help this problem? How can we deal with another's anger after we have understood the reason for it?

3. ***Identify the Skill Components:*** (List on board before class.)

    1. Listen and stay calm.
    2. Think of the consequences of different behaviors.
    3. Ask why the other party is angry.
    4. Make suggestions as to how to help the situation.
    5. If you are also becoming angry, leave for awhile.
    6. If one behavior doesn't work, try another.

4. ***Model the Skill:*** Select a situation from a popular T.V. show where one character is angry. Teacher and student will role play. Teacher will show understanding of student's anger and will calmly deal with it.

5. ***Behavioral Rehearsal:***

    A. ***Selection:*** Ask for four pairs of students to role play.

    B. ***Role Play:*** Use the following situations for role play. Students may have an opportunity to reverse roles if there is time.

    — A student has been told that someone else said that he/she wants to fight.

    — A student has been hit by a spitball and thinks that you threw it. The student is very angry with you, however, you are innocent.

164

— You have just received your report card. You have made the honor role, but your best friend has earned all Cs, Ds and Fs. He is very angry.

— The teacher is angry because someone plugged the sink with paper and left the water running to deliberately flood the classroom. She/he thinks you did this. You have tried to defend yourself. No one believes you. You are about to be suspended upon the recommendation of the teacher.

C. ***Completion:*** After each role play, reinforce correct behavior, identify inappropriate behaviors, and reenact role play with corrections. If there are no corrections, role play is complete.

D. ***Reinforcers:*** Verbal praise for correct choices while role playing.

E. ***Discussion:*** Discuss with the class why there is so much anger and violence and how it is shown in society (radio, TV, news). If people understood the reasons for anger, could they learn how to deal with it more peacefully?

6. ***Practice:*** Distribute copies of the following activity sheet "Understanding Another Person's Anger" to the class. After students have listed the five skill steps, ask them to turn over the paper and write about a situation where understanding another's anger could have prevented more trouble.

7. ***Independent Use:*** Ask students to track their improvement in understanding another's anger. Let them write down situations that occur outside the classroom. Have them return these reports to class for discussion.

8. ***Continuation:*** Teachers should continue pointing out the need to remain calm when someone else becomes angry.

CHILDREN'S LITERATURE

Start a class book club and encourage students to read rather than watch T.V. Some excellent authors for this level include Betsy Byars and Lois Lowry.

Name _____ Date _____

UNDERSTANDING ANOTHER PERSON'S ANGER

If someone is angry with me, I must do six things. Please list these things.

1. _____

_____

2. _____

_____

3. _____

_____

4. _____

_____

5. _____

_____

6. _____

_____

If I do the things that I just wrote, then I *will not fight!*

ACCEPTING CHANGE

SOCIAL SKILL
Accepting Good or Bad Changes

Behavioral Objective: The student will be able to understand and accept changes whether good or bad. When the student learns to accept changes, it will help to prepare him/her for a better life in the future.

Directed Lesson:

1. **Establish the Need:** Change is often difficult to accept, but is unavoidable in life. Like feelings, change can make one either happy or sad. It is necessary to accept changes that make one sad and learn to create better things in the future to regain happiness.

2. **Introduction:** The teacher tells a story about a boy who broke his leg playing baseball. The boy had to change in many ways. He had to walk on crutches, stop playing baseball, give up swimming, etc. Discuss how the student felt. What would happen to the student's attitude and behavior if he couldn't accept the change? If he accepts the change, what new things can he learn to do?

3. **Identify the Skill Component:** (List on board before class.)

    1. Understand that change may be unavoidable.

    2. Realize that everyone experiences change.

    3. Accept that change sometimes must occur.

    4. Recognize that change can be exciting.

4. **Model the Skill:** The teacher relates a story of teaching a lion raised in captivity to return to the wild. Discuss changes which will have to occur in the lion's behavior so that he/she can survive. He/she now has to catch food, defend him/herself against other animals and men, find shelter, etc. What would happen if the lion could not accept these changes or adapt to his/her new environment?

5. **Behavioral Rehearsal:**

    A. **Selection:** Select three different students for each role play situation, one of the students to act as teacher.

    B. **Role Play:**

    — Teacher gives surprise quiz.

    — An assignment that was due on Friday will not be due until Monday.

    — Gym has been canceled for the week.

    C. **Completion:** After each role play, reinforce correct behavior, identify inappropriate behaviors, and reenact role play with corrections. If there are no corrections, role play is complete.

    D. *Reinforcers:* Verbal praise, nonverbal approval (smile, pat, hug).

    E. *Discussion:* Students will discuss the role plays and any inappropriate behaviors that needed corrections. Discuss the difficulties of change and the need to be flexible in most situations.

6. *Practice:* Distribute copies of the following activity sheet entitled "Changes Collage" to students. They are to cut out pictures representing changes (e.g., new building, hairstyles, etc.) from magazines or newspapers to make a collage.

    To complete the collage as a group activity, use posterboard.

7. *Independent Use:* Teacher distributes the activity sheet "Changes at Home" and asks students to follow directions.

    These reports should be returned in one week to be discussed in class.

8. *Continuation:* Teachers should continue pointing out the need for accepting changes in all aspects of our lives.

Name _____ Date _____

CHANGES COLLAGE

Directions: Create a collage showing changes. Use cutouts from magazines or newspapers. (*Examples:* a new building, vacations, hair styles, new baby.)

* *

* *

Name _____ Date _____

CHANGES AT HOME

Directions: Using complete sentences, describe three changes that have occurred in your home in the past year and describe your reactions to these changes.

1. _____

_____

_____

_____

2. _____

_____

_____

_____

3. _____

_____

_____

_____

ACCEPTING CHANGE

SOCIAL SKILL
Reacting to Change

Behavioral Objective: The student will understand and accept changes whether positive or negative.

Directed Lesson:

1. **Establish the Need:** Teacher discusses with the class the fact that everyone in life experiences change. Nothing remains the same; therefore, we must learn to accept changes throughout our life whether they are good or bad.

2. **Introduction:** The teacher reads the following story to the class:

   > "Philip was a very popular student in school. He was also the captain of the basketball team, and president of his class. His family was experiencing financial problems in trying to make ends meet. His father received a promotion on his job that would enable him to take better care of his family. However, there was one catch to the promotion. The family had to move from New York City to a rural town in North Carolina. When Philip was told by his parents that they would be moving in a couple of months, he stormed out of the house."

   Ask the following questions:

   1. Why did Philip react the way he did?
   2. Should his father make this move?
   3. Did you ever think something was going to turn out bad, and it turned out to be a very pleasant experience? (Share)
   4. Because you're moving to another place, does it have to be a bad experience?
   5. How should Philip try to react to this change in his life?

3. **Identify the Skill Components:** (List on board or write on sentence strips.)

   1. Think about your feelings.
   2. Think about the reason(s) for the change.
   3. Realize that you can adapt to change.
   4. Be able to anticipate change.
   5. Accept the change, and go on to the next project.

4. **Model the Skill:** Teacher will model the skill steps after reading the following situation to the class.

171

"The fifth grade class was anticipating a field trip to the amusement park. Many students had gotten together to decide on who would bring certain food for the outing. All of the students were talking about the thrilling rides they would be experiencing. The day before the trip, the principal came to the class, and announced that the school board would not permit field trips to amusement parks, therefore, the trip had to be cancelled."

5. ***Behavioral Rehearsal:***

   A. ***Selection:*** Teacher selects two students for each role play situation.

   B. ***Role Play:*** Choose one student to role play the teacher, and the other student to go through skill steps.

      — *Teacher:* "Boys and girls, the physical education teacher is absent today, therefore no gym class."

      — *Teacher:* "Class, due to electrical problems, lunch will be delayed an hour."

      — *Teacher:* "Class, there will be no outside recess today because of the bad weather."

   C. ***Completion:*** After each role play, reinforce correct behavior, identify inappropriate behaviors, and reenact role play with corrections. If there are no corrections, role play is complete.

   D. ***Reinforcers:*** Verbal encouragement, group reinforcements, verbal praise, material rewards.

   E. ***Discussion:*** Have students discuss the role plays and the corrections that were made. Ask class why it is important to be able to accept change.

6. ***Practice:*** Distribute copies of the following activity sheet entitled "Changes From Life in a Skyscraper to Life in a Farmhouse."

7. ***Independent Use:*** Have the class survey five people outside school about their reactions to change, using the following "Survey Sheet." Discuss the findings in class one week from today.

8. ***Continuation:*** Teacher should continue to point out the need for each of us to adapt to changes as related situations arise.

Name _____ Date _____

CHANGES FROM LIFE IN A SKYSCRAPER TO LIFE IN A FARMHOUSE

Directions: Use the skill steps to help Philip adapt to his new environment.

_____

_____

_____

_____

_____

_____

_____

_____

_____

_____

_____

_____

_____

Name _____ Date _____

SURVEY SHEET

Directions: Survey five people to see how they react to the following changes.

Reactions to Changes

Moving

1. _____

2. _____

3. _____

4. _____

5. _____

Teacher being absent

1. _____

2. _____

3. _____

4. _____

5. _____

Special class being cancelled

1. _____

2. _____

3. _____

4. _____

5. _____

SOCIAL SKILL
Adjusting to Change

Behavioral Objective: The students will learn to understand and accept change. This will prepare them for a better life in the future.

Directed Lesson:

1. ***Establish the Need:*** Teacher initiates discussion about accepting change at home and in the classroom. She/he explains that when we do not accept changes graciously, it can cause unhappiness, misunderstanding, anger, and frustration. It is important that the students understand that change may be unavoidable.

2. ***Introduction:*** Discuss with the class the following situation: The sixth grade class had been eagerly looking forward to Wednesday. Their teacher had promised to bring in a camcorder to tape the play the class had been practicing for the last month. On Wednesday, the class was greeted by a substitute teacher. She/he explained that the taping would have to be postponed.

3. ***Identify the Skill Components:*** (List on board.)

    1. Accept that change is sometimes unavoidable.

    2. Choose or accept an alternate activity.

    3. Adjust to changes gracefully.

4. ***Model the Skill:*** The teacher relates an incident from his/her own experience when change was unavoidable. The teacher then tells how he/she reacted to the change in a positive way. He/she then asks class to brainstorm some changes that could occur and positive ways to react to them.

5. ***Behavioral Rehearsal:***

    A. ***Selection:*** All students will take part.

    B. ***Role Play:*** Ask students to recall changes in their lives where they reacted in a positive way. Call on individuals to help think of other ways the students could have reacted positively in those situations.

    C. ***Completion:*** After each role play, reinforce correct behaviors, identify inappropriate behaviors, and reenact role play with corrections. If there are no corrections, role play is complete.

    D. ***Reinforcers:*** Verbal and nonverbal praise.

    E. ***Discussion:*** Discuss how positive reactions to changes can help the students in their everyday lives.

175

6. ***Practice:*** Distribute copies of the following crossword puzzle. Have students complete the puzzle independently in class and then compare answers and discuss. Answers are as follows: 1. Change; 2. Happiness; 3. Choice; 4. Accept; 5. Adapt; 6. Substitute; 7. Understand; 8. Unavoidable.

7. ***Independent Use:*** Give students copies of the activity sheet entitled "My Reactions to Change." Instruct them to take the activity sheet home, complete it, share it with an adult at home, have the adult sign it, and then bring it back to school. Students and teachers will then discuss the activity sheets.

8. ***Continuation:*** Teacher should continue pointing out the need for adjusting to change in all phases of our lives in and out of school.

Name _____ Date _____

CROSSWORD PUZZLE

Choose a word from the work bank to complete the sentence. Print the word in the correct puzzle space.

Word Bank

accept

adapt

change

choice

happiness

substitute

unavoidable

understand

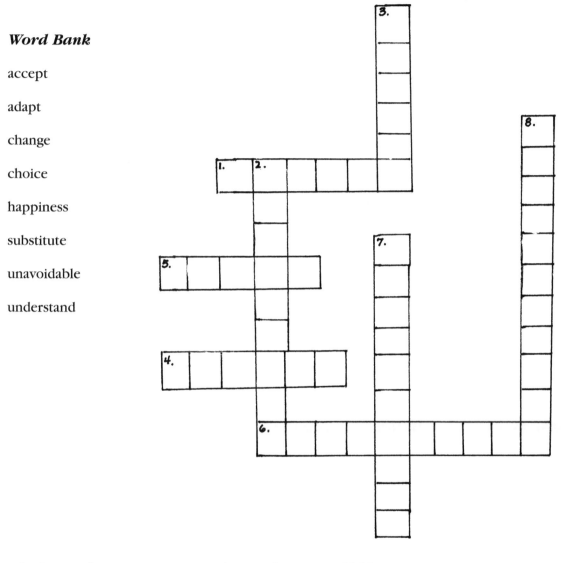

1. Accept that _____ is sometimes unavoidable.

2. Adjusting to change gracefully leads to _____.

3. There is always another _____.

4. We should learn to _____ a change.

5. To be happy, we must learn to _____ to change.

6. _____ an alternate activity.

7. Try to _____ the reason for a change.

8. Some changes are _____.

Name _____ Date _____

MY REACTIONS TO CHANGE

You are faced with the following situations. Write a few sentences to describe your POSITIVE reactions to each experience.

A. YOUR FAMILY IS MOVING TO ANOTHER TOWN.

_____

_____

_____

B. YOUR BEST FRIEND FINDS ANOTHER FRIEND AND NO LONGER HAS TIME FOR YOU.

_____

_____

_____

C. YOUR PET DOG RUNS INTO THE STREET AND IS KILLED.

_____

_____

_____

D. YOUR PARENTS ARE GETTING A DIVORCE.

_____

_____

_____

_____

(Parent's Signature)

DEALING WITH FEELINGS

SOCIAL SKILL
Showing That We Care

Behavioral Objective: The student will tell persons that he/she understands how others feel, and in some way show that he/she understands their feelings in an acceptable manner.

Directed Lesson:

1. ***Establish the Need:*** Discuss with the class the need for understanding how another person feels. Ask, **"Why do we need to understand other people's feelings?"** (*Sample responses:* to show we care; to show understanding; to make them feel better, etc.) **"What might happen if we didn't show people that we understand how they feel?"** (*Sample responses:* You don't care about them; no concern for others.)

2. ***Identify the Skill Components:*** (List on board.)

   1. Think about a person's actions, sayings, expressions.
   2. Decide what feeling a person is showing.
   3. Ask the person how she/he feels.
   4. Do or say something to let the person know you understand.

3. ***Model the Skill:*** Teacher models the correct behaviors in the following situation: A student in his/her class has just received a low grade on a test, and says, "I thought I passed that test. Now I note that my grade is going down."

4. ***Behavioral Rehearsal:***

   A. ***Selection:*** Choose two students to role play each situation.

   B. ***Role Play:*** Place the following situations on index cards.

      — A student was teased about the way she came dressed to school.

      — A student came in last in the school's play day race.

      — A student spilled his lunch in the cafeteria.

   C. ***Completion:*** After each role play, reinforce correct behavior, identify inappropriate behaviors, and reenact role play with corrections. If there are no corrections, role play is complete.

   D. ***Reinforcers:*** Verbal praise, nonverbal approval, group reinforcement, material rewards.

   E. ***Discussion:*** Discuss and review results of role plays.

5. ***Practice:*** Distribute copies of the following activity sheet, "How Would You Feel?" for students to complete in class. Discuss their responses.

6. ***Independent Use:*** Have students write about a feeling they might have shown at home or some member of their family might have shown, and how understanding was shown to them or by them for another person.

7. ***Continuation:*** Teachers should continue pointing out the need for demonstrating our concern for others as related situations arise.

Name _____ Date _____

HOW WOULD YOU FEEL?

Directions: For each situation below, tell how you might feel and how you would want to be treated.

1. You are the new student at school.

   _____

2. When you went to the store, an older boy stole your money.

   _____

3. On the way to school, you lost your lunch money.

   _____

4. In gym, you were the last one to be chosen for a team.

   _____

5. Your team lost the kickball game.

   _____

6. You received the lowest grade on the spelling test.

   _____

7. You had to take a note home about your behavior at school.

   _____

8. You read a report in front of the class for the first time.

   _____

9. Your younger brother or sister goes everywhere with your parents.

   _____

10. You have a math problem that you can't figure out.

   _____

Find These Feeling Words

sad	happy
proud	upset
angry	anxious
confused	alone

A	B	Z	H	A	P	P	Y	A
C	O	N	F	U	S	E	D	N
B	O	N	K	P	Z	I	E	X
U	W	Z	L	R	M	O	A	I
P	B	I	I	O	E	F	L	O
S	A	D	E	U	N	S	O	U
E	G	H	I	D	K	L	N	S
T	A	N	G	R	Y	O	E	W

SOCIAL SKILL

Demonstrating Sportsmanship

Behavioral Objective: The student will show in a positive manner that he/she understands another person's feeling in regard to sports and games.

Directed Lesson:

1. **Establish the Need:** Review with the class the importance of understanding another's feelings especially in games and sports. Discuss with them the meaning of "sportsmanship." *Example:* One who plays fairly and wins or loses gracefully. Ask what might happen if a person did not have good sportsmanship? Responses might be arguments, fights, penalties, etc.

2. **Introduction:** Teacher reads the following situation:

   "The big day was finally here. Room 205 and Room 102 were going to play each other in the Kickball Tournament. Both teams practiced their skills, and were excited about winning. Both teams played hard, and everyone was given a chance to play regardless of their skill ability. Well, Room 102 lost. The students in Room 205 knew how it felt to work hard and lose. So all class members in Room 205 went to persons in Room 102 and told them that they had played a good game and shook their hands."

3. **Identify the Skill Components:** (List on boards.)

   1. Think about the game sportsmanship.
   2. Think about your feelings when you win or lose.
   3. Show the other person(s) you understand their feelings.
   4. Act the way you would want to be treated.

   Have the class look at the skill components on the board and note whether those steps were shown in the story.

4. **Model the Skill:** Teacher models the skill by choosing a student to role play how one should act when they have won a game and when they have lost a game.

5. **Behavioral Rehearsal:**

   A. **Selection:** Choose volunteer students to role play the following:

   B. **Role Play:**

   — Two students in a spelling contest: One spells a word wrong, the other wins the contest.

182

— Two students in a race: One comes in last, the other is the winner.

C. ***Completion:*** After each role play, reinforce correct behavior, identify inappropriate behaviors, and reenact role play with corrections. If there are no corrections, role play is complete.

D. ***Reinforcers:*** Nonverbal encouragement (smile, pat on back, hug), verbal praise, student reinforcement, material rewards.

E. ***Discussion:*** Discuss role play results. How well were the steps followed?

6. ***Practice:*** Distribute copies of the following activity sheet entitled "Sportsmanship" for students to complete in class or at home.

7. ***Independent Use:*** Have students tell about an experience they had either in school or at home where they did or should have shown good sportsmanlike conduct when playing games or sports.

8. ***Continuation:*** Teachers should remind students of the importance of demonstrating sportsmanship in all kinds of competitive situations.

Name _____   Date _____

SPORTSMANSHIP

Directions: Tell how you would feel and act towards others in the following situations:

1. Both you and your friend were in a physical fitness clinic, but your friend was chosen to compete, not you.

   _____

2. Your family was playing a board game, and your younger brother kept losing.

   _____

3. At lunchtime some of the girls in your class were playing a game of Jacks. A girl you didn't particularly like kept losing.

   _____

4. On Fun Day at your school, your class was competing against another class in relay racing. The other class lost.

   _____

5. During a game in gym, you couldn't make the basket to help your team win.

   _____

Decode the following message using the order of the alphabet. That is, 1 = A, 2 = B, 3 = C, and so on.

19 8 15 23   21 14 4 5 18 19 20 1 14 4 9 14 7   15 6

1 14 15 20 8 5 18 19   6 5 5 12 9 14 7 19

_____   _____   _____

_____   _____

Having good sportsmanship enables everyone to have an enjoyable time.

SOCIAL SKILL
Recognizing Another's Emotions

Behavioral Objective: When presented with someone showing obvious signs of an emotion or mood, the student can learn to recognize the emotion or mood and to express the feelings in words.

Directed Lesson:

1. **Establish the Need:** Teacher will discuss with students that sometimes our behavior is affected by our feelings, which can be seen through the various moods and emotions we express. In order to get along with others, we must learn how to recognize and understand others' feelings.

2. **Identify the Skill Components:** (List on board.)

    1. Look at the person.
    2. Decide what you think the person is feeling.
    3. Ask the person if he/she is feeling the way you think.
    4. Tell the person you would like to help.
    5. Leave the person alone until he/she asks for help.

3. **Model the Skill:** Demonstrate various emotions nonverbally, such as anger, happiness, sadness, etc. Tell the students what mood you are showing and how they might be able to distinguish between different moods by noting body language.

4. **Behavioral Rehearsal:**

    A. **Selection:** Teacher will have three students role play moods or emotions while other students identify the mood or emotion.

    B. **Role Play:**
    — Student starts crying after teacher returns paper.
    — Student runs into the room laughing and clapping his/her hands.
    — Student slams book shut and throws away paper.

    C. **Completion:** After each role play, reinforce correct behavior, identify inappropriate behaviors, and reenact role play with corrections. If there are no corrections, role play is complete.

D. ***Reinforcers:*** Material rewards, verbal praise, nonverbal expression of approval (smile, pat, hug), group reinforcement.

5. ***Practice:*** Distribute copies of the following activity sheet entitled "What Emotions Do You See?" for students to complete and discuss in class.

6. ***Independent Use:*** Students can be made aware of how they can use this skill in the lunchroom, playground, at home, and elsewhere.

7. ***Continuation:*** Teachers should point out the value of recognizing others' feelings in all our relationships with one another.

Name _____ Date _____

WHAT EMOTIONS DO YOU SEE?

Directions: List five things a person might do when he or she is mad.

1. _____

2. _____

3. _____

4. _____

5. _____

Directions: List five things a person might do when he or she is sad.

1. _____

2. _____

3. _____

4. _____

5. _____

Directions: List five things a person might do when he or she is angry.

1. _____

2. _____

3. _____

4. _____

5. _____

Directions: On a separate piece of paper, tell how *you* might respond to each behavior.

SOCIAL SKILL
Respecting Others' Viewpoints

Behavioral Objective: Students will respect the differing views and behaviors of others in a positive, socially acceptable manner.

Directed Lesson:

1. **Establish the Need:** This skill is necessary for effective communication between the student and others in society.

2. **Introduction:** The teacher will discuss the following examples in regard to respecting others' rights and ways in this country (U.S.A.).

   — Jehovah's Witnesses' right not to pledge allegiance to our flag.

   — Muslims' way of covering their heads and women wearing a dress or skirt at all times.

   — School authority's right to expect us to observe school rules.

3. **Identify the Skill Components:** (List on board before class.)

   1. Listen quietly to another's views.

   2. Analyze the speaker's feeling and speech.

   3. Respond in a socially acceptable way.

4. **Model the Skill:** The teacher will role play the skill by presenting a situation in which he/she behaves in some way that is not generally accepted in the U.S.A.

5. **Behavioral Rehearsal:**

   A. **Selection:** Teacher selects student for role play.

   B. **Role Play:** Students role play situations in which they:
      — Dress differently.
      — Eat different foods.
      — Speak different languages.

   C. **Completion:** After each role play, reinforce correct behavior, identify inappropriate behaviors, and reenact role play with corrections. If there are no corrections, role play is complete.

   D. **Reinforcers:** Material rewards, verbal praise, group reinforcement.

   E. **Discussion:** Students will discuss the necessity of accepting persons of different cultural backgrounds while allowing them to maintain their ethnic heritage.

6. ***Practice:*** Distribute copies of the following activity sheet entitled "Two Viewpoints" for students to complete and discuss in class.

7. ***Independent Use:*** Have students tell of a situation outside of school where they should respect another's opinion.

8. ***Continuation:*** Teachers should continue to point out the need for respecting others' differing views as related situations arise.

CHILDREN'S LITERATURE

Polacco, Patricia. *The Keeping Quilt.* NY: Simon & Schuster, 1988.

_____. *Thundercake.* NY: Philomel, 1990.

Do a Patricia Polacco author study and read many multicultural tales by this author.

Name _____ Date _____

TWO VIEWPOINTS

Think of a situation where two people have different views but respect each other's opinion or view. Draw in a cartoon with speech balloons that depicts this situation. Use all four boxes.

DEALING WITH FEELINGS

SOCIAL SKILL
Apologizing When at Fault

Behavioral Objective: The student will apologize when he/she is at fault.

Directed Lesson:

1. **Establish the Need:** This skill is useful so that conflict does not become aggressive. Teacher tells the class that apologizing can prevent conflicts from getting out of hand. If you apologize first, the other person may be too ashamed to continue the argument.

2. **Introduction:** The teacher reads the following situation to the class.

    "Sue let Mary borrow her new bracelet. Mary wore the bracelet at recess and it got scratched."

    Using the skill steps listed on the board, when Mary returns the bracelet to Sue, what should she do and say?

3. **Identify the Skill Components:** (List on board before class.)

    1. Decide if you are at fault.
    2. Apologize if you are at fault.
    3. Apologize without being coaxed.

4. **Model the Skill:** Teacher will borrow something (pencil) from a student and pretend to break it. Teacher tells how to apologize. (Replace the pencil.)

5. **Behavioral Rehearsal:**

    A. **Selection:** Teacher selects students for each role play.

    B. **Role Play:** Have three students use the role plays listed below dealing with when and how to apologize. Together the class can then make up three situations where students would need to apologize and use them as additional role plays.

    — John accidentally stepped on Joe's toe in the lunch line.

    — You forgot to sweep the kitchen floor.

    — You forgot to tell your mother about an important phone message.

    C. **Completion:** After each role play, reinforce correct behavior, identify inappropriate behaviors, and reenact role play with corrections. If there are no corrections, role play is complete.

      D. ***Reinforcers:*** Verbal praise, nonverbal expression of approval, group reinforcement.

      E. ***Discussion:*** Students discuss positive and negative aspects of role-play apology and the necessity for being sincere when making an apology.

6. ***Practice:*** Distribute copies of the following activity sheet entitled "How to Apologize" and have students complete it together in class.

7. ***Independent Use:*** Have students keep a tally during one week and have it signed by the person who they apologized to; i.e., I'm sorry for _____. Have students bring the tally to class for discussion.

8. ***Continuation:*** Teachers should continue pointing out the need to apologize when at fault as related situations arise.

Name _____ Date _____

HOW TO APOLOGIZE

Directions: Below are scrambled words with a box for each word. *First,* unscramble all the words and write each one in its own box. *Next,* match a word in Row 1 with a word in Row 2 to produce an expression used in an apology. *Finally,* write these five expressions on the five lines beneath the two rows.

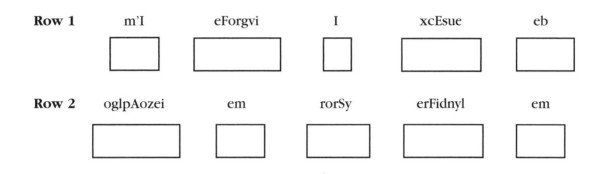

Row 1   m'I   eForgvi   I   xcEsue   eb

Row 2   oglpAozei   em   rorSy   erFidnyl   em

	Row 1	Row 2
1.		
2.		
3.		
4.		
5.		

SOCIAL SKILL
Complimenting Others

Behavioral Objective: The student will express positive feelings about another person by means of a compliment.

Directed Lesson:

1. ***Establish the Need:*** Everyone needs to feel good concerning the things they are doing. Complimenting is a way to tell people that they're doing something well and that they should keep up the good work they are doing.

2. ***Introduction:*** The teacher reads the following situation to the class.

> **"On a Friday during art class, Room 114 was making paper bag puppets. One boy, Marco, did not like art that much because he could not color well. However, he liked puppets and decided to be extra careful when coloring today. He had been working awhile when Tina said to him, 'Marco, you are really coloring nicely today, using all kinds of colors.' He didn't know what to say at first since he rarely received a compliment. A few seconds later he said 'Thanks,' and continued his work. Marco was glad someone noticed that he was doing a super job."**

Discuss these questions.

1. How did Marco feel about the compliment?
2. Are there other reasons why Marco may have disliked art?
3. Give the compliment in an unforced and sincere tone of voice.

4. ***Model the Skill:*** Teacher models skill by giving each student a deserved compliment.

5. ***Behavioral Rehearsal:***

   A. ***Selection:*** Using pictures, artwork, or good photographs, the teacher will select five students and give a compliment to each one.

   B. ***Role Play:*** The teacher will select five students to give a compliment about another student the teacher has also selected. The compliment might relate to a way of dressing, behavior, academic work, special projects, or hobbies. Reinforce correct behaviors and compliment those sincerely.

   C. ***Completion:*** After each role play, reinforce correct behavior, identify inappropriate behaviors, and reenact role play with corrections. If there are no corrections, role play is complete.

    D. ***Reinforcers:*** Verbal praise, material rewards, group reinforcement.

    E. ***Discussion:*** The students should discuss the role plays and state why compliments are deserved.

6. ***Practice:*** Distribute copies of the following activity sheet entitled "Understanding Feelings" for students to complete and discuss in class.

7. ***Independent Use:*** Ask students to give a compliment to some of the people they know outside school and at home. Students should write down the compliments for the teacher to see and discuss.

8. ***Continuation:*** Teachers should continue pointing out the need to compliment others for their good work and kindnesses.

Name _____ Date _____

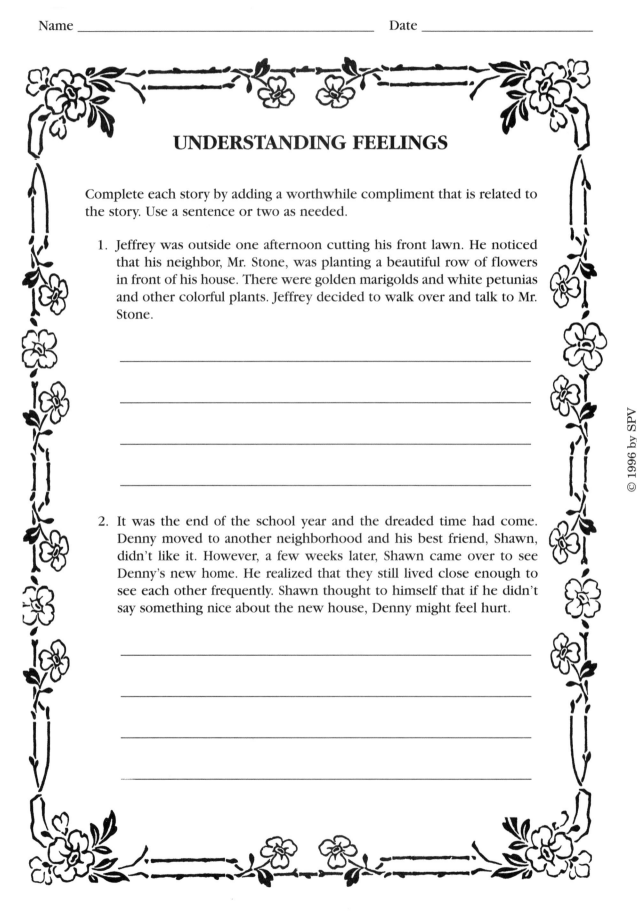

UNDERSTANDING FEELINGS

Complete each story by adding a worthwhile compliment that is related to the story. Use a sentence or two as needed.

1. Jeffrey was outside one afternoon cutting his front lawn. He noticed that his neighbor, Mr. Stone, was planting a beautiful row of flowers in front of his house. There were golden marigolds and white petunias and other colorful plants. Jeffrey decided to walk over and talk to Mr. Stone.

   _____

   _____

   _____

   _____

2. It was the end of the school year and the dreaded time had come. Denny moved to another neighborhood and his best friend, Shawn, didn't like it. However, a few weeks later, Shawn came over to see Denny's new home. He realized that they still lived close enough to see each other frequently. Shawn thought to himself that if he didn't say something nice about the new house, Denny might feel hurt.

   _____

   _____

   _____

   _____

SOCIAL SKILL
Practicing Active Listening

Behavioral Objective: The student will use active listening skills to interpret feelings being expressed.

Directed Lesson:

1. **Establish the Need:** Discuss the importance of understanding feelings. How can we learn to become more understanding? Active listening is the answer. This is a way of learning to empathize. To fully understand another person, you have to be able to walk in the shoes of that person, as the saying goes. Empathizing is important for making friends and keeping them.

2. **Introduction:** Discuss with the class the meaning of empathizing with others and how valuable a skill this is and how to learn to empathize. To master this skill will enlarge your circle of friends.

3. **Identify the Skill Components:** (List on board before class.)

    1. Listen with attention, interest, caring.
    2. Listen for information AND FEELINGS.
    3. Tell the speaker what you think he/she said and wanted to convey.
    4. Ask the speaker if you heard correctly and understood.

4. **Model the Skill:** Teacher asks the class who of the students has a "pet peeve" she/he would like to share with the teacher in front of the class. Teacher models each step of active listening as the class observes and charts her/his behavior (see the following "Observer's Chart: Active Listening Behavior" activity sheet). After a few examples are modeled, the teacher asks the student to be the active listener and another to tell a "pet peeve." The class observes and charts the behavior. After each role play, ask the speaker how it felt to be listened to in that way.

5. **Behavioral Rehearsal:**

    A. **Selection:** This may be a whole class or small group activity.

    B. **Role Play:** PLAN A: Divide the class into groups of three. One student tells a "pet peeve," one practices active listening, and a third charts behavior. Roles are rotated. PLAN B: Form a large circle. Appoint a student to be the active listener. Each member of the class who wishes to share a "pet peeve" may do so, as the student who is leading the group practices active listening. Appoint a third student to chart the behaviors.

    C. ***Completion:*** After each role play, reinforce correct behavior, identify inappropriate behaviors, and reenact role play with corrections. If there are no corrections, role play is complete.

    D. ***Reinforcers:*** Class comments on the positive skills of the leader/listener at the end of the session.

    E. ***Discussion:*** Review the role playing and discuss the students' observations. How does active listening help us understand feelings more clearly?

6. ***Practice:*** Use the following "Observer's Chart: Active Listening Behavior" activity sheet for "teacher modeling" and for "role playing." Instead of listening to stories on "pet-peeves," other stories should be used such as happiness, birthday, promotion, loss of job, etc.

7. ***Independent Use:*** Discuss with students the impact they have on all of the younger students in the school. Many of the smaller students would like to have contact with older students. Suggest that students devise a character, a hero, in puppet form (e.g., "Caring Clyde" or "Understanding Unger") who could visit the primary classrooms with a "Little Boy" puppet and a "Little Girl" puppet and show how the "hero" listens and understands the feelings of the other two puppets. Invite the primary students to use the girl or boy puppet to tell a feeling that they have. A puppet show could be given in the classroom for primary students. An extra set of puppets might be left with the primary teacher to use.

8. ***Continuation:*** Stress the necessity for active listening in truly understanding how another person thinks and feels.

CHILDREN'S LITERATURE

Creech, Sharon. *Walk Two Moons.*

This 1995 Newbery-award winner ties in with the concept in the "Establish the Need" on the previous page. It invites the reader to "walk two moons" in another's moccasins. An excellent read-aloud book for this level.

Name _____ Date _____

OBSERVER'S CHART: ACTIVE LISTENING BEHAVIOR

Note: The purpose of this chart is to record *what the observer is seeing* so that he/she can become a sharper observer. No one is expected to exhibit ALL of these behaviors in the process of active listening. Each active listener will develop responses that feel natural and authentic to him/her.

Names of Persons Being Observed

Makes eye contact							
Nods where appropriate							
Smiles where appropriate							
Leans toward speaker							
Focuses attention without interruption							
Retells important information							
Expresses feelings of speaker							
Uses an inquiring tone of voice							
Looks directly at speaker							
Tries to put ideas into own words							
Other:							
Other:							

Note: The purpose of this chart is not to "grade" the listener, but to sharpen YOUR observation skills.

SOCIAL SKILL
Identifying Emotional Tones

Behavioral Objective: Each student will be able to describe the emotional content in a spoken message.

Directed Lesson:

1. **Establish the Need:** We often communicate as much with the emotional tone of our voice as with the words themselves. Being able to read these emotional tones is a very important skill.

2. **Introduction:** Teacher says to class: **"Is it possible to say exactly the same words but mean two quite different things? Let's take an example: Each of these two students will, in the next minute, come up to tell me that he/she needs help. But I will whisper something to them that will make their needs extremely different ones. See if you can figure out the nature of the help needed, just by watching and listening to the WAY each says the identical words. "I need help."** Teacher whispers to one that he is in great pain, to the other he is slightly confused about a math problem. Do this experiment and others.

3. **Identify the Skill Components:** (List on board before class.)

   1. Attend to the tone of voice, expression on face, and gestures of the body when interpreting the feelings in a message.

   2. Ask the speaker if you interpreted his/her feelings correctly.

4. **Model the Skill:** Teacher asks the class to help brainstorm many feelings that may color a spoken message, such as disgust, fear, sorrow, scorn, disappointment, confusion, pride, regret, anticipation, resentment, etc. Teacher models ways in which these emotions may be conveyed without saying, "I feel afraid." Teacher chooses a phrase such as "I see the flowers." and says it with a variety of different emotions. Class must guess which feeling she/he is expressing by watching her/his expression, gestures, and tone of voice.

5. **Behavioral Rehearsal:**

   A. **Selection:** Ask for voluntary participants. The number of students will vary according to the time and speed of role play.

   B. **Role Play:** Distribute pieces of paper on which feeling words are written. Each student who wishes to participate comes to the front of the room and repeats the same sentence, voicing it with emotion. Class must guess the emotion and check it out with the speaker.

C. ***Completion:*** After each role play, reinforce correct behavior, identify inappropriate behaviors, and reenact role play with corrections. If there are no corrections, role play is complete.

D. ***Reinforcers:*** If emotion was obviously portrayed, the class will guess it easily. Congratulate those students with verbal praise and with applauding.

E. ***Discussion:*** Point out how some students portrayed their emotions more obvious and easier to guess. What can we do with this information? How can understanding another's feeling help us get along better?

6. ***Practice:*** Have students read a story from their reading book. Have them select a character to express vocal emotions when speaking to the class. How would the voice sound? Have everyone in the class write this information on a piece of paper and discuss.

7. ***Independent Use:*** Students will report a scene from a selected T.V. show in which a character displays vocal emotional feelings. Students will discuss their interpretations of the character's emotions. Students can also write about an incident that involved a family member's emotional tone of voice when dealing with the student. These observations are to be discussed in class one week from today.

8. ***Continuation:*** Teachers should continue pointing out the value of being able to detect emotional tone variations in a speaker's voice.

CHILDREN'S LITERATURE

Introduce the students to *The Magic School Bus* series by Joanna Cole and Bruce Degan. Videotapes of these fascinating stories are also available from the public library. Listen carefully to the children's voices for emotions "behind the words."

SOCIAL SKILL
Expressing Understanding

Behavioral Objective: The student will learn to express how he/she understands another's feelings in acceptable ways.

Directed Lesson:

1. **Establish the Need:** Create a situation such as someone's being very sad because of a friend's death. Perhaps someone teased the person about his/her sad expression. Talk with the class about how they would feel if they had been in such a situation. Decide how you could help understand and express the sad person's feelings.

2. **Introduction:** Teacher tells this story to the class:

   "One day Carla came to school with a very sad expression on her face. When Terry noticed her expression, he began to laugh at her and call her names. He did not ask her why she was sad. Mr. Smith, the teacher, called Terry to the desk and said that his behavior was unacceptable. He explained that Carla's father was to have a serious operation and she was naturally upset. Later, Mr. Smith found out that Terry had teased Carla again."

   Discuss what you think should happen next.

3. **Identify the Skill Components:** (List on board before class.)

   1. Think what the person is feeling.
   2. List your ideas quietly.
   3. Think about your ideas.
   4. Offer your help and express your understanding.
   5. Try alternative ideas.

4. **Model the Skill:** Teacher shows students pictures depicting people in different moods and students will tell how they should react to the various people.

5. **Behavioral Rehearsal:**

   A. **Selection:** Teacher selects students for role play.

   B. **Role Play:** Let students share magazine pictures and divide them into groups. Later have the various groups reveal their findings to the rest of the class. Permit the students to practice the steps.

C. ***Completion:*** After each role play, reinforce correct behavior, identify inappropriate behaviors, and reenact role play with corrections. If there are no corrections, role play is complete.

D. ***Reinforcers:*** Awards, peer tutoring, verbal praise.

E. ***Discussion:*** Students will discuss why it is important to understand how another person feels at a given time and how understanding another person's feelings can assist you in helping the person.

6. ***Practice:*** Distribute copies of the following activity sheet entitled "What Are They Feeling?" for students to complete and discuss in class.

7. ***Independent Use:*** Ask students to make a special effort to befriend at least one person whom they think needs his/her feelings understood. Share with the class their success rate and what they did when they succeeded and how difficult it was.

8. ***Continuation:*** Teachers should remind students of the importance of showing understanding of others' feelings in all of our daily activities and interactions with other people.

Name _____ Date _____

WHAT ARE THEY FEELING?

Directions:

1. Find pictures of various people in magazines.

2. Cut out pictures and attach them to this page.

3. What do you think each person is feeling? Write a descriptive word by each picture.

4. Discuss this with a partner or with other classmates.

SOCIAL SKILL
Recognizing Individual Differences

Behavioral Objective: The student will be able to recognize, accept, and appreciate individual differences.

Directed Lesson:

1. **Establish the Need:** The teacher initiates a discussion about the relevance and benefits of the skill. It is important to display tolerance for an individual who has characteristics different from our own by accepting him/her without derogatory comments or actions.

2. **Introduction:** The teacher tells the class that a new student will be joining the class. The new student is a unique individual because he is purple. Discuss reactions to a purple person. Does it make a difference? How do you feel? Do you think you could be friends?

3. **Identify the Skill Components:** (List on board before class.)

    1. Identify individual differences.
    2. Treat everyone with respect.
    3. Include everyone in your activities.
    4. Recognize that everyone is unique.

4. **Model the Skill:** A foreign exchange student from Egypt comes to the class. She speaks English with difficulty and dresses differently. Teacher will model greeting her and introducing her to the class.

5. **Behavioral Rehearsal:**

    A. **Selection:** Teacher selects four students to role play different situations using the following role play.

    B. **Role Play:** A young parrot comes to the pet shop. He has a speech defect which makes him hard to understand. Other parrots are approaching him for the first time. The parrots have a hard time understanding him, but they all try and eventually play together.

    C. **Completion:** After each role play, reinforce correct behavior, identify inappropriate behaviors, and reenact role play with corrections. If there are no corrections, role play is complete.

    D. **Reinforcers:** Verbal praise, nonverbal approval (smile, pat, hug).

    E. **Discussion:** How do you feel when you are excluded from a game? Why were you excluded? Have you ever excluded anyone? Why? Discuss empathy and respect for others. Discuss positive attitudes and individual differences; everyone is unique.

6. ***Practice:*** Distribute copies of the following activity sheet entitled "Word Search" for students to complete in class.

7. ***Independent Use:*** Give students copies of the activity sheet entitled "Different Times" to do at home. After completing the activity on front of the worksheet, they are to write a story on a separate sheet of paper or on back of the worksheet as directed. Students will bring their work back to class for discussion.

8. ***Continuation:*** Teachers should continue pointing out the need for accepting and appreciating individual differences in all of our daily contacts with others both in and out of school.

Name _____ Date _____

WORD SEARCH

Directions: Circle each letter of the clue words—up and down, forwards and backwards. Letters left over will spell an important message.

Clue Words:

prejudice	unique	differences
individual	respect	everyone
understand	appreciate	kind
appreciate	recognize	accept
characteristic	size	identify
friend		

a	p	p	r	e	c	i	a	t	e	e	z	i	s
c	h	a	r	a	c	t	e	r	i	s	t	i	c
c	i	d	e	n	t	i	f	y	e	v	e	r	y
e	v	e	r	y	o	n	e	u	q	i	n	u	b
p	d	n	e	i	r	f	t	c	e	p	s	e	r
t	o	d	d	n	a	t	s	r	e	d	n	u	y
e	c	i	d	u	j	e	r	p	i	d	n	i	k
s	i	n	d	i	v	i	d	u	a	l	u	n	i
q	s	e	c	n	e	r	e	f	f	i	d	u	e

Message:

_ _ _ _ _ _ _   _ _   _ _ _ _ _ _.

Name _____ Date _____

DIFFERENT TIMES

Directions: Examine the pictures. List the similarities and differences that you find.

Similarities   *Differences*

_____   _____

_____   _____

_____   _____

_____   _____

_____   _____

_____   _____

On a separate page, write a story using complete sentences. Tell about what might happen if a time machine brought a cave family into your house today. What would you need to teach the cave people about your culture?

DEALING WITH PREJUDICE

SOCIAL SKILL

Accepting Each Person's Uniqueness

Behavioral Objective: The student will learn that each person has unique qualities. The student will further learn to understand that while we are alike in many ways, we must accept each other for our individual differences.

Directed Lesson:

1. **Establish the Need:** "**People are different in many ways. We must learn to accept differences, and appreciate a person's individuality. People are also alike in several ways, and these likenesses as well as differences in people make our world exciting and interesting.**"

2. **Introduction:** Teacher initiates a discussion of the ethnic make-up of the United States. Emphasize the racial, religious, as well as cultural differences. Bring out the positive aspects of these differences such as variety of foods, entertainment styles, contributions to society, etc.

3. **Identify the Skill Components:** (List on board or write on sentence strips.)

    1. Think about the cultural differences.

    2. Say to yourself, "I will accept these differences because everyone is unique."

    3. Show respect for individual differences by understanding their importance to society.

4. **Model the Skill:** Teacher reads the following story to the class:

    "**A new family moved next door to Ann. This family had come from India. The father was a doctor, and would be working at the local hospital. The daughter enrolled at our school, and on the first day, she wore her native dress (which is called a sari).**" **Teacher then models skill steps to fit the story.**

5. **Behavioral Rehearsal:**

    A. **Selection:** Choose two students to role play each situation—total of six students.

    B. **Role Play:**

    1. *1st Student:* "Say Tom, how about coming over to my house for lunch. We're having pierogies."
    2nd Student: Follows skill steps.

    2. *1st Student:* "Mary is an American Indian, and she is going to be in your class. What do you think of that?"
    2nd Student: Follows skill steps.

3. *1st. Student:* "Say Michael, are you going to be in on the Xmas gift exchange? I hope I get your name."
   2nd Student: "No, my religion does not allow me to do that."
   1st Student: Follows skill steps.

C. **Completion:** After each role play, reinforce correct behavior, identify inappropriate behaviors, and reenact role play with corrections. If there are no corrections, role play is complete.

D. **Reinforcers:** Material rewards, verbal encouragement, group reinforcement.

E. **Discussion:** Students discuss the fact that everyone is uniquely different in some way. Students are then given a chance to identify their own unique qualities. Teacher explains, "Although we are different, we also have many things in common." Have students express the commonalities of people.

6. **Practice:** Distribute copies of the following activity sheet entitled "Dealing with Prejudices" and read through the directions with the class. Have students complete the worksheet independently in class and then share information.

7. **Independent Use:** Give students copies of the following home activity sheet, "The Aliens Have Landed." Have them explain the differences they see between the pairs, and apply the skill steps. Have them return the activity sheet within a week for class discussion.

8. **Continuation:** Teacher should stress the importance of accepting each person's uniqueness in all of our contacts with others.

Name _____   Date _____

DEALING WITH PREJUDICES

Directions: Describe how people are alike. Describe their differences.

Name _____ Date _____

THE ALIENS HAVE LANDED!

Directions: Identify the differences between each pair of aliens. Apply the skill steps.

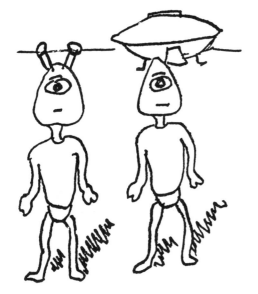

SOCIAL SKILL

Appreciating Our Differences

Behavioral Objective: The students will be able to recognize that although we are alike in many ways, we must accept and appreciate our individual differences.

Directed Lesson:

1. **Establish the Need:** The purpose is to show that uniqueness can be interesting as well as stimulating. To be able to make friends without prejudice and in fact be cooperative with persons who are different from oneself is the desired outcome.

2. **Introduction:** Briefly review (retell, if necessary) the story of Cinderella. Through the following questions and statements, direct the students to notice that the prince acted without prejudice:

    1. Describe Cinderella's family.
    2. What did her sisters think of her?
    3. Describe her everyday clothes.
    4. Where did the prince look for Cinderella?
    5. Who was allowed to try on the slipper?
    6. Do you think she was really changed by the Fairy Godmother? How?

3. **Identify the Skill Components:** (List on board before class.)

    1. Accept and/or recognize that everyone is different.
    2. Beware of first impressions.
    3. Look for the positive qualities in new acquaintances.
    4. Withhold judgment until you know a person.

4. **Model the Skill:** The teacher selects two students. Tell the class a complimentary fact about each one. Then ask the students how it felt to be described in that way. Afterwards ask the two students to state something positive about you, the teacher. Tell how you felt.

5. **Behavioral Rehearsal:**

    A. **Selection:** Arrange the whole class in groups of two.
    B. **Role Play:** Students take turns telling positive facts about each other and giving their reaction to these facts.
    C. **Completion:** After each role play, reinforce correct behavior, identify inappropriate behaviors, and reenact role play with corrections. If there are no corrections, role play is complete.

    D. ***Reinforcers:*** Teacher gives praise, verbal and nonverbal, and expressions of approval for those responses that indicate understanding of the skill.

    E. ***Discussion:*** Students will discuss the importance of getting to know another person before making judgment, and in this way learn to recognize the unique quality of others.

6. ***Practice:*** Divide the class into teams for a treasure hunt. Distribute copies of the following activity sheet entitled "Treasure Hunt" and allow a reasonable length of time for the groups to complete the search. Discuss special qualities about those that were discovered through this activity.

7. ***Independent Usage:*** Students should keep a daily record of people they have come in contact with for one week, and the new positive quality they have found in each person. Distribute the activity sheet "Positive Qualities." Have students complete it and then return the record to school and discuss it in class.

8. ***Continuation:*** Teachers should continue pointing out the need for recognizing and respecting individual differences in all of our dealings with others.

CHILDREN'S LITERATURE

Do a Cinderella study from different cultures. Secure the following books:

Young, Ed. *Lon Po Po,* A Chinese Cinderella Story. NY: Philomel, 1989.

Climo, Shirley. *An Egyptian Cinderella.* Illustrated by Ruth Heller. NY: Crowell, 1989.

Martin, Rafe. *The Rough-Face Girl,* An Algonquin Cinderella Tale. Illustrated by David Shannon. NY: Putnam's, 1992.

Name _____ Date _____

TREASURE HUNT

Directions: Find one person in the group who fits the description given. Put the name of that person beside the description. Do not use yourself for any of the items on your own sheet. Find a person in your group who:

1. flew in an airplane _____

2. has two living grandparents _____

3. knows how to make pudding _____

4. has a baby brother or sister _____

5. has a birthday this month _____

6. collects stickers _____

7. plays piano or guitar _____

8. likes pizza with anchovies _____

9. sings in a choir _____

10. was born out of state _____

11. is not afraid of snakes _____

12. watches cable T.V. _____

13. earns own spending money _____

Name _____   Date _____

POSITIVE QUALITIES

Directions: Write the name of a different person and a new positive quality you have discovered about each one. Do this every day for one week.

Day	*Person*	*Positive Quality*
_____	_____	_____
_____	_____	_____
_____	_____	_____
_____	_____	_____
_____	_____	_____
_____	_____	_____
_____	_____	_____
_____	_____	_____
_____	_____	_____
_____	_____	_____
_____	_____	_____
_____	_____	_____
_____	_____	_____
_____	_____	_____
_____	_____	_____
_____	_____	_____

DEALING WITH PEER PRESSURE

Lesson 66

SOCIAL SKILL

Saying "No" to Negative Peer Pressure

Behavioral Objective: The student will respond to negative peer pressure by ignoring or demonstrating some other appropriate responses (e.g., walking away, changing the subject, calling for help).

Directed Lesson:

1. **Establish the Need:** Teacher will have the following discussion.

   "It is apparent that many students, children, grown-ups and adolescents are challenged by peers who display negative behavior. Students should be made aware of how to deal with the pressures of undesirable behavior in order to avoid their influence."

2. **Introduction:**

   1. Define negative peer pressure.
   2. Discuss inappropriate behavior (fighting, pushing, joining gangs, etc.).
   3. Discuss appropriate behavior (ignoring, walking away, only doing what is right, etc.).
   4. Discuss why students should use appropriate behavior.
   5. Discuss the consequences of inappropriate behavior.

3. **Identify the Skill Components:** (List on board.)

   1. Distinguish between right and wrong.
   2. Decide on the course of action.
   3. Ignore inappropriate peer pressure.
   4. Ask for help if you need it.

4. **Model the Skill:** Teacher will use a hypothetical situation in which his/her peers are trying to influence him/her to fight an adult who accidentally bumped into him/her.

5. **Behavioral Rehearsal:**

   A. **Selection:** Ask for volunteers. One at a time.

   B. **Role Play:** Arrange a variety of conditions so that many responses can be assessed.

   — Have a student role play being pressured into fighting by his peers.

   — Have another student role play ignoring his peer in order to avoid the fight.

   — Have students take different roles than the ones they usually display.

217

C. **Completion:** After each role play, reinforce correct behavior, identify inappropriate behaviors, and reenact role play with corrections. If there are no corrections, role play is complete.

D. **Reinforcers:** When appropriate behavior is displayed, reward students with kind words, a pat, a smile, tokens, material rewards, verbal praise, nonverbal expression of approval (i.e., smile, pat, hug), group reinforcement.

E. **Discussion:** Students should have an opportunity to discuss and evaluate the skill. Teacher should help direct students discussion by using leading questions such as (1) Why is this skill needed? (2) How would you feel if you were being beaten up? (3) How did the beating come about? (4) Could fighting be avoided?

Students can be motivated to participate in group discussion by having them imagine themselves in a certain situation. Let them discuss how they would handle the situation.

6. **Practice:** Distribute copies of the following activity sheet entitled "What's Your Decision" for students to complete and discuss in class.

7. **Independent Use:** Ask students to record how they are able to overcome negative peer pressure for one week. Have them bring these records to class for discussion.

8. **Continuation:** Teacher should continue pointing out the need for resisting negative peer pressure as related situations arise.

Name _____ Date _____

WHAT'S YOUR DECISION?

1. A friend wants to copy your homework. What do you say?

   _____

   _____

   _____

   _____

2. A group of friends want to pull the fire alarm. The friends want you to join them.

   _____

   _____

   _____

   _____

3. Your friend's older brother drinks some wine. He wants you and your friend to drink some too. He says, "C'mon, try some, then you'll be cool." Your friend takes some. What do you do?

   _____

   _____

   _____

   _____

4. Your classmates are planning to take the teacher's lunch. They ask you to stand guard. What will you do?

   _____

   _____

   _____

   _____

5. Your best friend has stolen $10.00. He wants to give you half of it. What should you do?

   _____

   _____

   _____

   _____

SOCIAL SKILL

Ignoring Negative Pressure

Behavioral Objective: The students will continue working hard regardless of peer pressure which tries to convince them to slow down.

Directed Lesson:

1. ***Establish the Need:*** Teacher will say to students, **"It is apparent that many students are influenced by peers who try to negatively influence them. Students who allow others to influence them not to work up to their academic potential may suffer short- and long-term effects. They cannot be recommended for special academic programs, nor for getting certain desired jobs, etc."**

2. ***Introduction:***

   1. Teacher will discuss the need and rewards gained by those who work up to their potential.

   2. Teacher and class discuss the appropriate motivation one needs in order to work up to one's potential. (Work neatly, finish work, listen, etc.)

   3. Teacher and class discuss some of the inappropriate behaviors that cause students not to work up to their potential.

   4. Teacher explains why student should demonstrate appropriate behavior. Consequences are discussed (you may fall further behind in subjects).

3. ***Identify the Skill Components:*** (List on board.)

   1. Ignore what others want you to do by using peer pressure.

   2. Think about the consequences.

   3. Decide what you want to do.

   4. Decide on how you will ignore negative peer pressure.

   5. Continue working.

4. ***Model the Skill:*** The teacher models the appropriate behavior. Showing the student alternatives he/she might use when peers are pressuring him/her not to do his/her work.

5. ***Behavioral Rehearsal:***

   A. ***Role Play:*** The students will role play a situation in which a boy has to decide if he's going to work up to his potential, which means aiming higher than his friends. If he chooses to aim higher, he has to accept criticism and isolation from those who think it is square and sissified to get high grades. Students should be given an opportunity to role play this situation to demonstrate both the appropriate and inappropriate responses.

    B. ***Reinforcers:*** When appropriate behavior is displayed, students are rewarded with kind words, pat, smile, free time, special jobs, material rewards, verbal praise, nonverbal expression of approval, group reinforcement, etc.

6. ***Practice:*** Distribute copies of the following activity sheet entitled "The Answer Is 'No'" for students to complete and share in class.

7. ***Independent Usage:*** Students will continue working at home even when their friends call and interrupt or the family wants to do other things. Students shall write about a situation that occurred, and describe how they were able to deal with the peer pressure. These situations should be brought to class for discussion.

8. ***Continuation:*** Teachers should point out the need for resisting negative peer pressure as related situations arise.

Name _____ Date _____

THE ANSWER IS "NO"

Directions: Write what you would say or do if someone tries to keep you from completing school work. Give the reason why.

Problem: Two older kids want you to play baseball with them when you have homework to do.

What Do You Do:

Why:

Problem: A friend starts to whisper to you in class while you are doing a math problems.

What Do You Do:

Why:

Problem:

What Do You Do:

Why:

Problem:

What Do You Do:

Why:

Problem:

What Do You Do:

Why:

SOCIAL SKILL
Saying "No" to Negative Group Pressure

Behavioral Objective: The student will walk away from peers using negative group pressure setting.

Directed Lesson:

1. ***Establish the Need:*** Discuss the idea of independent thinking which takes into account the concept of fairness. To follow the crowd often entails insufficient thinking about a situation and can lead to unexpected negative consequences.

2. ***Introduction:***

    A. The teacher will define the term "group pressure."

    B. The following story will be read to the class with questions to follow.

    "One day during lunch time at _____ School, Joseph was asked by his friends to steal a lunch from a third grader named Susan. Joseph, after thinking said, 'No because I don't want to get into trouble.' Then he walked away."

    1. What did the group want Joseph to do?

    2. How did Joseph react to group pressure?

    3. Name three things that Joseph did.

3. ***Identify the Skill Components:*** (List on board before class.)

    1. Listen to the group's request.

    2. Judge the request and weigh consequences.

    3. If you say "no," give a reason and walk away.

    4. Do so politely.

4. ***Model the Skill:*** Teacher will role play a situation in which he/she says no to group pressure when asked to participate in a negative group situation.

5. ***Behavioral Rehearsal:***

    A. ***Selection:*** Teacher selects groups of students for each role play.

    B. ***Role Play:*** The teacher can have students role play a few group-pressure situations of his/her own design similar to the story above.

C. ***Completion:*** After each role play, reinforce correct behavior, identify inappropriate behaviors, and reenact role play with corrections. If there are no corrections, role play is complete.

D. ***Reinforcers:*** Teacher will provide verbal and/or non-verbal praise.

E. ***Discussion:*** Students will discuss value of learning to say "no" to negative groups pressure and will also discuss the value of not placing pressure on friends unfairly.

6. ***Practice:*** After the role play, distribute copies of the activity sheet entitled "John's Dilemma" for students to complete in class.

7. ***Independent Usage:*** Give students copies of the following survey activity sheet "Lunchroom Survey" to complete on their own. The worksheet can be used to record the number of group-pressure incidents and especially incidents of food theft observed over the course of a week. Their findings should be compared, graphed, and discussed in class.

8. ***Continuation:*** Teachers should continue pointing out the need for resisting negative group pressure as related situations arise.

Name _____ Date _____

JOHN'S DILEMMA

John received a note today that read, "Meet our gang after school today. We're going to have a big fight." What should John do? Make a cartoon to show what happens. Use the skill steps.

Remember: Listen.
    Think about consequences.
    Decide.

Name _____ Date _____

LUNCHROOM SURVEY

To determine whether or not group pressure is present conduct a survey during lunch time. Look for the following types of behaviors.

1. Is anyone taking food without permission?

    a. Is food being taken from students?

    b. Is food being taken from food bins, crates, or counter?

2. Is the student being asked to do these things by a group or is he/she doing it on his/her own?

We will look carefully for these things and note them. Write them on paper. Do not write down any names. Also, look for the behavior of younger students, not just your own grade level. Do this for one week.

Day	Number of Incidents Seen	Number of Group Pressure Situations	Number of Individual Thefts

DEALING WITH PEER PRESSURE

SOCIAL SKILL
Resisting Negative Peer Pressure

Behavioral Objective: The student will walk away from a negative group-pressure setting.

Directed Lesson:

1. ***Establish the Need:*** Teacher and class discuss saying "no" when confronting situations in which they are asked to participate in something they know is wrong. This is necessary to avoid unpleasant situations.

2. ***Introduction:*** Teacher reads the following story to the class:

> **"Barbara and Joyce were walking home from school one afternoon when they noticed an elderly lady drop her wallet. Barbara picked up the wallet and saw that there was money in it. Joyce became excited and wanted to split the money and run home. Barbara, after thinking it over, decided that they would catch up to the woman and return the wallet with all of the money still in it."**

Have the class read and discuss the questions below.

   1. **What was the peer-pressure situation in this story?**
   2. **How did Barbara handle the pressure?**
   3. **Do you feel you would do as Barbara did? Why or why not?**

3. ***Identify the Skill Components:*** (List on board before class.)

   1. Listen to the peer's request.
   2. Judge the request and weigh consequences.
   3. Say "no," give a reason and walk away.

4. ***Model the Skill:*** Teacher will role play situation in which he/she says no and walks away from a negative peer-pressure setting.

5. ***Behavioral Rehearsal:***

   A. ***Selection:*** Teacher selects students for each role play.

   B. ***Role Play:*** Have students use the following situations for the role play.

   — Three students are walking past an unguarded soda truck.

   — Several students find a lost wallet in the lunchroom containing money.

   — Several students are trying to get you to leave school early.

C. ***Completion:*** After each role play, reinforce correct behavior, identify inappropriate behaviors, and reenact role play with corrections. If there are no corrections, role play is complete.

D. ***Reinforcers:*** Teacher and students offer verbal and/or nonverbal praise for appropriate behavior.

E. ***Discussion:*** Students should discuss the role play and decisions made by the class and the individual students.

6. ***Practice:*** Distribute copies of the following activity sheet entitled "Handling Peer Pressure" and do it together in class.

7. ***Independent Use:*** Have students list at least one incident where someone tried to involve them in a negative group/peer-pressure situation and they resisted. The incident can be something that happened in school or at home. The students should report back to class in one week for discussion.

8. ***Continuation:*** Teachers should continue pointing out the need and value of resisting negative group pressure whenever related situations arise.

Name _____ Date _____

HANDLING PEER PRESSURE

Directions: Read the story below and write an ending using the correct skill steps.

Two boys were throwing pebbles at a dog that was tied to a nearby tree. John came along and the boys shouted for him to throw pebbles too. If you were John, what would you do or say to the two boys?

_____

_____

_____

_____

_____

_____

_____

_____

Directions: Write your own peer-pressure story, and be sure to tell how you would handle the pressure.

_____

_____

_____

_____

_____

_____

_____

_____

_____

SOCIAL SKILL
Knowing Your Own Unique Qualities

Behavioral Objective: Student will be able to state a personal quality that is valued by himself/herself and not shared by members of his/her peer group.

Directed Lesson:

1. **Establish the Need:** Students need to understand that their own personal qualities are to be valued and will help them feel better about themselves. It is also more important to rely on one's own values than to be accepted by others.

2. **Introduction:** Read the picture book, *The Sneetches*, by Dr. Seuss. If this is not available, see the synopsis of the story accompanying this lesson. Discuss the two social groups in the Sneetch community: the IN group and the OUT group. How did members of the IN group *identify* themselves? (By the stars on their bellies) What do members of the IN group do to the Sneetches who do not conform? (Exclude them from their parties, snub them, etc.) Help students to see this story as a PARODY of group identity and group exclusiveness.

3. **Identify the Skill Components:** (List on board before class.)

   1. Think about the styles, attitudes, and behaviors that characterize your own social group. (These may be styles of clothing and hair, modes of walking or talking, or attitudes toward school, family, self.)

   2. Think of at least one style, attitude, or behavior you like about yourself that is not part of your group's identity.

   3. Think about why you like this attribute in yourself.

   4. Communicate this positive thinking and feeling in one of these ways: raise your hand and tell the class, tell a partner, write it down in your personal journal.

4. **Model the Skill:** The teacher shows some magazine advertisements portraying adults in ways he/she does not identify with. Perhaps one is a perfume ad advising a woman to "make an impression" by smelling good. The teacher may feel there are more important ways to "make an impression," if "making an impression" is in fact important at all. Perhaps the image is of a macho cowboy lighting up a cigarette and the teacher says masculinity does not always agree with this POPULAR IMAGE. Perhaps it is the message of several ads taken together: that the measure of a person is the way he/she looks, and the name on his/her jeans. Perhaps that image negates what the teacher feels is most important: namely what is inside the person. The teacher states the attribute of her/his peer group. The teacher tells the class why that attribute is prized by himself/herself.

5. ***Behavior Rehearsal:***

    A. ***Selection:*** Each student can participate in the role play. Ask for as many volunteers as possible.

    B. ***Role play:*** Encourage each student to think of one characteristic in himself/herself that is not part of the group image, but that is regarded very highly by him/her. Encourage the student to reason why his/her attribute is positive and of value.

    C. ***Completion:*** After each role play, reinforce correct behavior, identify inappropriate behaviors, and reenact role play with corrections. If there are no corrections, role play is complete.

    D. ***Reinforcers:*** Have the class verbally praise those students who were able to express their qualities that do not match with those of the peer group.

    E. ***Discussion:*** Teacher leads brainstorming of styles, attitudes, and behaviors that are urged by the student's peer group: punk style clothing, kind of jeans, self-defense training, using a particular expression or way of walking, style of greeting, or attitude toward school. Let the ideas come from the class.

6. ***Practice:*** Distribute copies of the following activity sheet entitled "I'm Unique" and have students complete it individually in class. Share the information if there is time.

7. ***Independent Use:*** Distribute the activity sheet "A Summary of *The Sneetches* by Dr. Seuss and ask the class to write its own creative version(s) of *The Sneetches* using a different social convention (instead of star bellies and plain bellies, one custom that truly reflects peer-group identity in the school). The students will share their version(s) with another class, if appropriate, with their family, and their own class for discussion.

8. ***Continuation:*** Teachers should point out the need for each of us to recognize and express our own special qualities.

Name _____ Date _____

I'M UNIQUE

● Lots of kids in my age group follow these customs:

☞ fashions _____
(hair, jewelry, hats, etc.)

☞ expressions _____

☞ things to like/dislike _____

☞ attitudes/feelings _____
(school, goals, ways to be cool)

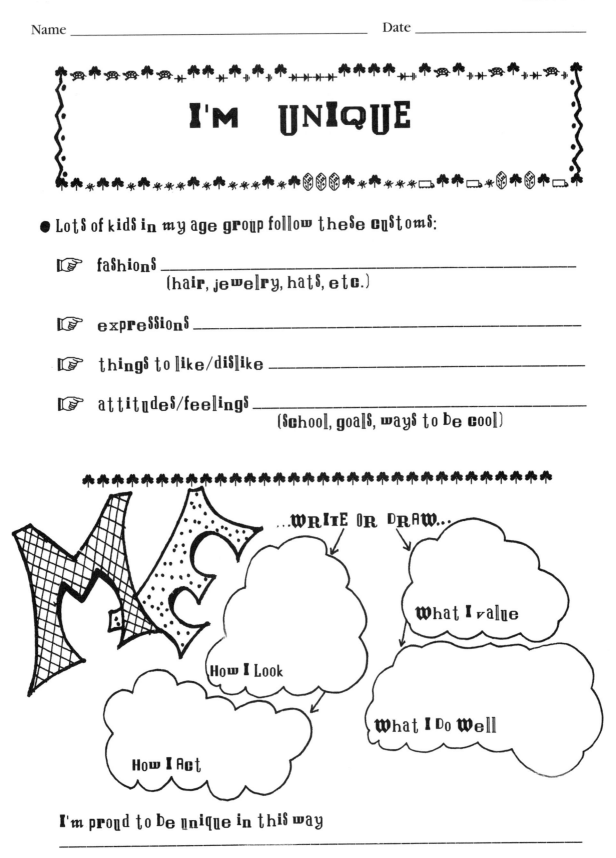

...WRITE OR DRAW...

How I Look

What I value

How I Act

What I Do Well

I'm proud to be unique in this way
_____

I think it's important because _____

Name _____ Date _____

SUMARY OF *THE SNEETCHES* BY DR. SEUSS

The Star-Belly Sneetches are the BEST on the beaches. They have parties, frankfurter roasts, and lots of games, to which the Plain-Belly Sneetches are never invited. To have a star on the belly is to be IN! One day a clever and enterprising huckster named Sylvester McMonkey McBean comes to town advertising his star printing machine. For a tidy sum he will place a star on the poor, plain belly on any Plain Belly Sneetch. There is great rejoicing among the Plain Bellies and great outrage among the Star Bellies. When all distinctions are erased, their prestige and privilege is gone. For a tidier sum, he will *remove* the star from any belly. Things get into a terrible confusion, with Sneetches tearing in and out of the STAR-ON MACHINE and the STAR-OFF MACHINE, and getting poorer all the time. When the last dollar is spent, McBean pulls out of town, declaring that silly Sneetches will never learn. Fortunately, the Sneetches do profit from experience and learn to get along with or without a star upon their bellies.

DEALING WITH PEER PRESSURE

SOCIAL SKILL
Learning to Think Independently

Behavioral Objective: The student will learn not to succumb to group and peer pressure.

Directed Lesson:

1. ***Establish the Need:*** Discuss peer pressure as it relates to antisocial behavior as expressed in gangs and gang behavior. Show that succumbing to this type of behavior can cause much unhappiness. This can result in academic underachievement and antisocial behavior. However, by thinking independently and not becoming a part of this gang mentality, the student can improve his/her academic and social standing in school and the community. Show the validity of being accepted by a socially adept group and note the benefits.

2. ***Introduction:*** Tell the students about being an accessory to a crime. Explain that being in the presence of those involved in crime still makes one involved. Elicit other stories from the students that come from their own experiences.

3. ***Identify the Skill Components:*** (List on board before class.)

    1. Listen carefully to suggestions from peer groups.
    2. Ask questions about issues you don't understand.
    3. Think carefully about consequences.
    4. Make a decision.
    5. Decide how important rejection will be to you.
    6. Think of other activities you could participate in that are acceptable.

4. ***Model the Skill:*** The teacher will role play situations where he/she pretends he/she is a student and must resist pressure to break group rules.

5. ***Behavioral Rehearsal:***

    A. ***Selection:*** Select or ask for five pairs of volunteers to role play.
    B. ***Role Play:*** One student in the pair will role play trying to pressure the other into doing something that is known to be wrong. If there is time, have them switch roles.
    C. ***Completion:*** After each role play, reinforce correct behavior, identify inappropriate behaviors, and reenact role play with corrections. If there are no corrections, role play is complete.
    D. ***Reinforcers:*** Have the class reinforce proper role play with positive comments.
    E. ***Discussion:*** Discuss the role playing and how well the students were able to avoid peer pressure that would hurt them. Review the steps needed to avoid peer pressure.

6. ***Practice:*** Distribute copies of the following activity sheet entitled "Peer-Pressure Situations." Ask the students to complete the activity sheet and share their methods and thinking on how to avoid the pressure to do something wrong.

7. ***Independent Use:*** Ask family members, teachers, and other adults who work with your students to reinforce the procedures used for avoiding involvement with gang behavior that is unacceptable. Ask students to report situations that occur outside of school where they have been able to avoid pressure to do wrong. Have them write a report on their experience with gangs to share it in class and discuss.

8. ***Continuation:*** Teachers should stress the importance of thinking independently and resisting a "herd mentality," as related situations arise.

Name _____   Date _____

PEER-PRESSURE SITUATIONS

Directions: How could you handle each situation so that you would feel good about yourself? Write your responses below or on back if more room is needed.

1. A student is thought to have taken all the new pens from the other students. Therefore the group is trying to get the majority to agree to beat up this student. What do you do when asked to help?

   _____

   _____

2. A student wants some small toys from the store but has no money. The group urges him/her to steal. What does the student do?

   _____

   _____

3. A student sneaks food from the lunchroom and causes the class not to be selected as THE BEST LUNCH BUNCH. There is group pressure to start a fight with that student. What do you do?

   _____

   _____

4. Some students have been "accidentally" pushing other students. The group being pushed is urging to form a gang and challenge others to a fight. You don't want to be involved, but your friends want you to help and will think you are a chicken if you do not fight. What do you do?

5. One student is constantly called "stupid" by another class member who also accuses him of having family problems. Upset, the student has trouble learning. His friends say he should just cut class. But the student knows how important education is. What should he do?

   _____

   _____

Lesson 72

SOCIAL SKILL
Preventing the Spread of Rumors

Behavioral Objective: The student will learn to avoid creating bad feelings for any person, especially members of their peer group.

Directed Lesson:

1. ***Establish the Need:*** Students should understand that it is necessary to stop a rumor and console the person who is damaged. It is also necessary to recognize that the person who started or repeated the rumor has special needs.

2. ***Introduction:*** Have you ever been accused of something you didn't do? Why were you accused? How did you react? How did you feel? Have you ever started a rumor about someone else? Why? How did the other person feel when they heard the rumor?

3. ***Identify the Skill Components:*** (List on board before class.)

    1. Ignore rumors.
    2. Encourage others to ignore rumors.
    3. Never start false rumors.
    4. Starting rumors hurts others and yourself.

4. ***Model the Skill:*** The teacher will model the skill by relating a rumor he/she was told. The teacher demonstrates how to stop a rumor from spreading.

5. ***Behavioral Rehearsal:***

    A. ***Selection:*** Teacher selects three students to role play various situations.

    B. ***Role Play:*** Students "W" and "X" begin talking about school. Student "Y" comes up and tries to overhear the conversation. When this fails, Student "Y" goes to Student "Z" and starts a rumor. Teacher should ask the class the following questions about the role play situation: What should Student "Z" do? How does "Y" feel? If "W" and "X" are told the rumor and who started it, how do they feel? What should they do?

    C. ***Completion:*** After each role play, reinforce correct behavior, identify inappropriate behaviors, and reenact role play with corrections. If there are no corrections, role play is complete.

    D. ***Reinforcers:*** Verbal praise, nonverbal approval (smile, pat, hug).

    E. ***Discussion:*** Discuss the fact that rumors can be detrimental to others. There is a difference between character assassination and a discussion about people in a positive manner.

6. ***Practice:*** Distribute copies of the following activity sheet entitled "Stopping a Rumor" for students to complete and discuss in class.

7. ***Independent Use:*** Give students copies of the activity sheet entitled "Don't Spread Rumors" to complete independently at home and return in one week to discuss in class.

8. ***Continuation:*** Teachers should continue pointing out the importance of stopping rumors as related situations arise.

Name _____ Date _____

STOPPING A RUMOR

Directions: Describe a situation in which your friend is trying to start a rumor. Include how you would stop it and how each person felt.

A. What is the rumor your friend is trying to start?

_____

_____

_____

_____

B. How would you stop the rumor?

_____

_____

_____

_____

_____

_____

_____

C. How do people in your situation feel?

_____

_____

_____

_____

_____

_____

Name _____ Date _____

DON'T SPREAD RUMORS

Directions: Analyze the pictures below and explain why it is important not to spread rumors.

1. _____
   _____
   _____
   _____
   _____
   _____
   _____
   _____
   _____
   _____
   _____
   _____

I heard that **Tiger** stole your food.

That is just a rumor! I will NOT spread it !

I saw Mama feeding the crow kids. She likes them better than us.

That's just a rumor!

2. _____
   _____
   _____
   _____
   _____
   _____
   _____
   _____
   _____
   _____
   _____
   _____

SOCIAL SKILL
Preventing False Rumors

Behavioral Objective: The student will learn to recognize a false rumor and develop strategies to prevent them in order to avoid creating bad feelings with anyone, especially members of their peer group.

Directed Lesson:

1. **Establish the Need:** Teacher will lead a discussion about the meaning of a false rumor, and the consequences brought about because of them. False rumors can be negative to a person's character as well as cause serious problems.

2. **Introduction:** Discuss the following questions: "Did anyone tell a rumor about you or someone you know?" Invite students to share their experiences. "How did the person feel when he or she heard the rumor? What were the results? Let's describe the type of person who would start a false rumor. Why do false rumors get started?"

3. **Identify the Skill Components:** (List on the board or place on sentence strips.)

   1. Never start a false rumor.
   2. Avoid listening to rumors.
   3. Say, "That's a false rumor and I'm not going to listen to it."
   4. Do not repeat rumors.
   5. Tell others to ignore rumors.
   6. Walk away.

4. **Model the Skill:** Teacher selects a student to read the following: **"Mrs. Taylor, did you hear what they're saying about Johnny?"** Teacher then demonstrates how to use the skill steps to stop the rumor.

5. **Behavioral Rehearsal:**

   A. **Selection:** Teacher selects two students to role play each situation.

   B. **Role Play:**

   Situation #1—*1st Student:* **"Paul told Joey that Tom said he was going to fight with him after school."** *2nd Student:* **"I'm not going to listen to that rumor or repeat it because someone could get hurt."** (Student then walks away.)

   Situation #2—*1st Student:* **"Ann, did you tell Sue about what happened to Sharon on the playground?"** *2nd Student:* **"No, I never spread rumors, and you shouldn't either because someone's feelings could get hurt."** (Student walks away.)

241

C. ***Completion:*** After each role play, reinforce correct behavior, identify inappropriate behaviors, and reenact role play with corrections. If there are no corrections, role play is complete.

D. ***Reinforcers:*** Verbal praise, self-praise, group reinforcement.

E. ***Discussion:*** Have students discuss the role-play situations. How did the participants feel while performing? Were the steps followed for stopping rumors? Why is it important to stop rumors?

6. ***Practice:*** Distribute copies of the following activity sheet entitled "Stopping False Rumors." Have students complete the activity and share their responses.

7. ***Independent Use:*** Give students copies of the activity sheet entitled "Rumor Busters Interview." Students must interview other students to complete the activity sheet. Have a follow-up discussion of their findings in class.

8. ***Continuation:*** Teacher should remind students of the harm caused by false rumors and the necessity of stopping them as related situations arise.

Name _____ Date _____

STOPPING FALSE RUMORS

Fill in the cartoon bubbles below to help stop false rumors!

Name _____ Date _____

RUMOR BUSTERS INTERVIEW

Directions: Choose three students to interview.

Questions:

1. What should you do when you hear a false rumor?

2. How do you feel when you are the victim of a false rumor?

3. What can you do to stop false rumors?

4. What harm is done when false rumors are passed on?

_____

_____

_____

_____

_____

_____

_____

_____

_____

_____

_____

_____

_____

_____

_____

_____

STOPPING FALSE RUMORS

SOCIAL SKILL

Preventing Spreading of False Rumors

Behavioral Objective: The students will be able to recognize rumors and develop strategies to prevent them.

Directed Lesson:

1. **Establish the Need:** Teacher defines rumor (a story or comment in circulation without confirmation of facts). A discussion follows on how to recognize rumors and their consequences. Students should be helped to understand and identify with the feelings of others.

2. **Introduction:** Read the following story:

   "Once a man became angry with his friend. To get even, he made up a hateful story about his friend and told this story to some people who told it to others. When he realized the harm he had done, he went to a wise man for advice on how to undo the damage. The wise man told him to take a sack of feathers with him to the bridge and empty the sack into the wind. Then he was to gather all the feathers back into the sack. Of course, he could not accomplish the task, so he returned to the wise man. The wise man then explained that once a rumor was circulated, it too was impossible to retract." The teacher then tells the students, "Since rumors are so hard to retract, it is important to stop them before they spread. How can we do this?"

3. **Identify the Skill Components:** (List on board before class.)

   1. Avoid listening to rumors.
   2. Do not spread rumors.
   3. Think of the feelings of the person about whom the rumor is being spread.
   4. Ask yourself if you would want that rumor spread about you.

4. **Model the Skill:** Teacher models the skill by telling of a rumor he/she heard and then squelched. She/he then asks students how else the situation could have been handled.

5. **Behavior Rehearsal:**

   A. **Selection:** Teacher selects two students to role play.

   B. **Role Play:** The role play is a telephone conversation where one student tells a rumor to the other and the second student handles it according to the behavior skills learned. Stress that persons' names not be used.

245

    C. ***Completion:*** After each role play, reinforce correct behavior, identify inappropriate behaviors, and reenact role play with corrections. If there are no corrections, role play is complete.

    D. ***Reinforcers:*** Verbal praise, nonverbal praise, class reinforcement.

    E. ***Discussion:*** Students will discuss the importance of avoiding listening to rumors, and developing strategies to prevent them from spreading.

6. ***Practice:*** Have students demonstrate their ability to squelch rumors effectively by completing the following "Telephone" activity sheet and discuss it in class.

7. ***Independent Use:*** Distribute copies of the following "'Rumor Doomer' Badge" activity sheet for homework. Return the completed badge to class within one week to share with the teacher and peers.

8. ***Continuation:*** Teachers should continue pointing out the need for stopping and preventing rumors from spreading whenever related situations arise.

Name _____ Date _____

TELEPHONE

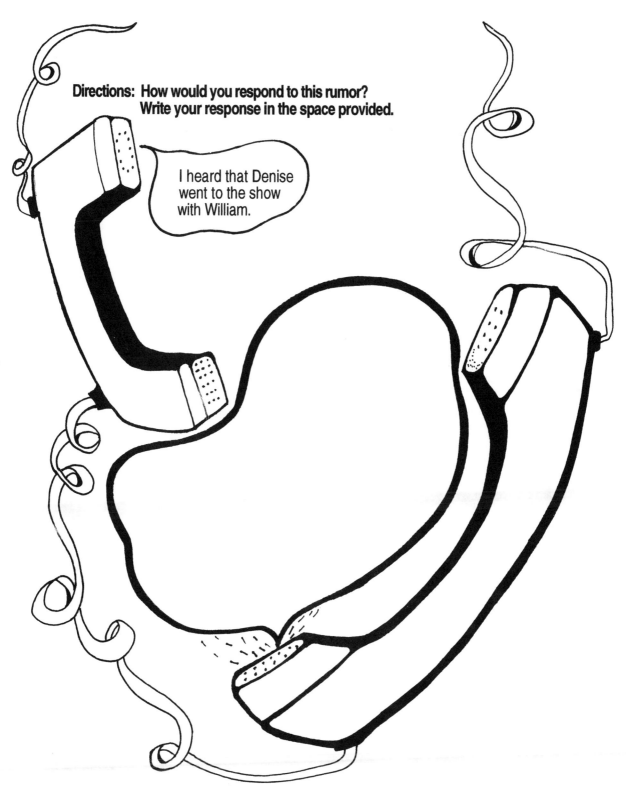

Directions: How would you respond to this rumor?
Write your response in the space provided.

I heard that Denise went to the show with William.

Name _____ Date _____

"RUMOR DOOMER" BADGE

You have a special challenge. Design a colorful badge that sends a visual message to STOP SPREADING RUMORS.

Part I presents 27 social skills-related topics on cards for teacher-led class discussions during Circle Time. Each topic can be introduced once before studying a particular skill, such as listening, and later after the lesson, to assess student's learning.

Note: The topics are printed in the form of discussion cards which can be photocopied and cut out for use at the appropriate time.

SOCIAL SKILLS TASK REVIEW

Part I

Why are social skills important?

Social skills are important because their frequent use and application determines how well we get along with other people.

What are they?

respect for others   *kindness*
listening   *politeness*
following directions   *self-control*
sharing   *cooperation*
consideration   *patience*
caring   *problem solving*
accepting change   *conflict solving peacefully*

Listening is important because. . .

Listening is important because if we do not listen when other people speak to us, we will never learn what they are telling us or know how to do something they may be showing us.

We need to listen carefully at these times:

Fire drill
When teacher gives a listen signal
When teacher gives directions
Any time teacher or family have to say something

Completing assignments is important because. . .

It is important to finish any job that you choose or are given in order to learn how to do things and how to do them well.

Discuss the importance of finishing things we start. The format can be, "What would happen if ⎮ "

- the road was only half finished
- the school bus had a flat tire that wasn't fixed
- the pizza was only half cooked, etc.

Why is it important to pay attention and not let other things distract you?

It is important to pay attention to what we are doing so that we can finish our work and learn how to do things.

What are we learning at school?

- how to use the computer
- how to put things away between classes
- how to sit quietly and listen to a speaker, etc.
- how to make friends
- how to solve problems (conflicts) peacefully
- how to be helpful to others
- how to use courtesy words such as please and thank you

It is important to follow instructions and directions because . . .

It is important to follow directions or instructions from your teacher or parents in order to prevent mistakes or accidents and to learn how to do things correctly and safely.

Why do we *walk* indoors and *run* outdoors?

Whose advice do you trust? Why?

Ex.   **I trust my mother's/father's/other relatives' advice because she/he loves me and has my best interests at heart.**

What advice do we give to someone who is

- crossing the street
- holding a pet
- being called by a stranger
- being talked to by a stranger, etc.

How do you settle conflicts without violence?

Ex.   **We can talk about the problem and try to reach a compromise.**
We can ask someone else to listen to both sides of the conflict
and tell us what they think is fair.
One of us can give in to the other or negotiate a different solu-
tion.

How can you avoid getting into a fight?

Ex.   **I can avoid getting into a fight by controlling my anger.**
I can stop and count to ten when I feel myself growing very
angry.
I can tell my teacher/relative about the problem instead of
fighting.

It takes a lot of practice to learn to handle conflicts constructively. Let's try these
things today:
(1)   **Think before you speak.**
(2)   **Speak in a quiet voice no matter how angry you may feel inside.**

Why is it important to be a good sport and accept consequences in a graceful manner?

Ex. **It shows that you are a good sport.**
It sets a good example for others.
It makes you a better person.
It keeps you from fighting and getting hurt.
It teaches you to follow the rules.

How do you react when you fail at something?

Ex. **I feel disappointed and frustrated.**
I promise myself that I will try again and succeed the next time.
I am embarrassed.
I will try to learn from failing not to fail again.

What we think about ourselves is very important. What do you *think* when someone tells you that you did a very good job?

Ex. **I think they are complimenting me on my good work.**
I think they are encouraging me to keep up the good work.
I think I will try harder to do good work.
I think . . .

How do you *feel* when someone tells you that you did a very good job?

Ex. **I feel proud of myself.**

I feel good about myself.

I feel happy that my work pleases them.

I feel . . .

How can we show understanding of another's feelings?

Ex. **When someone is hurt we can . . .**

When someone is crying we can . . .

When someone falls down we can . . .

When someone spills something we can . . .

It helps to talk over feelings with other people you trust. If you felt bad about something, who could you talk with?

Ex. **I could talk about it with my mom/dad because she/he would understand how I felt and help me feel less bad.**

Who else can we talk to? At home? At school?

How do you feel when you get a deserved compliment? How can we compliment others? Let's try. We can begin with the words:

"I like the way _____"
"I like it when _____"

It is important to ask permission politely if you want to borrow anything. Why? How can we put it into words and use the words today?

Ex.   **It is important to ask permission politely to borrow someone else's property because the more polite you are, the more likely they will let you use it.**

Ex.   "May I use the computer?"
         "May I play basketball, too?"
         "May I . . ."

Suppose we had a day when five of us felt angry. What could we do to try to make it a good day?

Ex.   **We could ask the five angry students to explain their feelings and see if there is some way to help them feel less angry.**

We can   walk away   tap our toes ten times

              hum a tune   count to ten

              look at a book   etc.

When someone gets angry with you, what are some ways that you can deal with their anger?

Ex. **I can talk to the person in a quiet voice.**
I can avoid getting angry myself.
I can count to ten.
I can try to calm the person by talking.
I can try to negotiate.

What things make you angry?

Ex. **I get angry when someone takes my belongings without asking me.**
I get angry when someone pushes ahead of me in the line.
I get angry when someone cheats in a game.

OK. So we feel mad. How can we "use our words" to tell about the anger rather than using our body?

Ex. **We can say in a quiet voice what we think is wrong and what should be done to make it right. We should find a solution that pleases both sides.**

What is positive peer pressure?

Positive peer pressure is being asked by friends or others to do something that is all right to do and that you may enjoy doing.

Ex.   **. . . to play a game of baseball**
             . . . to have dinner at their houses
             . . . to go to the movies with them

How do I react to positive peer pressure?

Ex.   **You may decide to do something if you are free and like doing it.**
         You may say "No thanks" if you have other more important or enjoyable things to do.
         You may simply say "Yes, I'd like to do that."

What is negative peer pressure?

Negative peer pressure is being asked by friends or others to do something that is wrong to do or something you do not like to do.

Ex.   **. . . to make fun of another person**
             . . . to steal something that belongs to someone else
             . . . to hurt an animal or another person

How do I react to negative peer pressure?

Ex.   **You may just say "NO!" in a nice way.**
        You may say, "Sorry, but I have other things to do."
        You may tell them that you think it's the wrong thing to do
        and not for you.

How do you feel about violence?

Ex.   **I think violence is wrong because it hurts others and doesn't**
        solve any problems.
        I think violence only causes hatred and leads to more violence.
        I think violence happens when people get too fearful and emo-
        tional and do not think before they act.

How do you feel about nonviolence?

Ex.   **I think nonviolence is the only way to settle arguments and**
        solve problems between people.
        I think nonviolence is the only way to achieve real and lasting
        peace among people.

SOCIAL SKILLS TASK REVIEW

Part II

Directions: Display the following social-skills-related words on a colorful chart with a catchy title such as that used in the example on the following page.

Discuss one word with the students each day. Then review the words using a procedure such as one of these:

- Have students use a pointer, point to a word, and explain what it means.

- Have a student point to a word and ask one of his/her classmates to tell what the word means.

- Give the meaning of a word and ask a student to point to the correct word.

Words	*Sample Explanation*
Social Skills	what we need to get along with others
Conflict	a disagreement in ideas or interests
Attitude	how we think and act about someone or something
Compromise	an agreement in which each side gives up some demands or desires
Listening	to pay attention to what others are saying
Self-Image	how we think and feel about ourselves and our abilities
Values	what we and others think are important and desirable to have
Peer Pressure	what our friends and peers want us to do
Negative Peer Pressure	what our peers want us to do but what is not right to do
Violence	fighting, shooting, hitting, and more
Nonviolence	discussing, talking quietly, and more

SOMETHING TO TACKLE

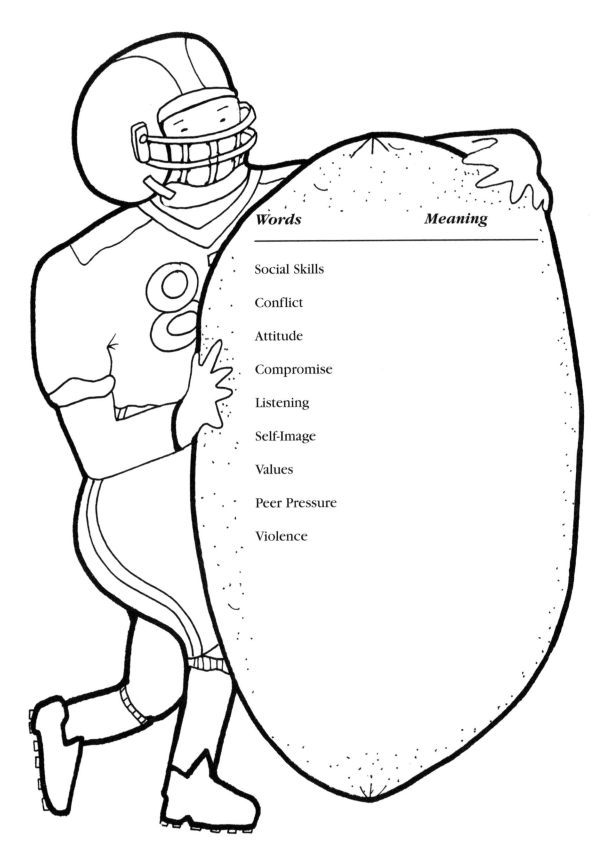

Words   **Meaning**

Social Skills

Conflict

Attitude

Compromise

Listening

Self-Image

Values

Peer Pressure

Violence

SOCIAL SKILLS
FAMILY TRAINING BOOKLET

The following pages present a social skills family training booklet entitled "Partners in Social Skills: A Family Affair" preceded by a "Family Letter" that introduces the booklet and can be signed by each child. The letter provides a good way to involve parents in the social skills development program to coordinate home and classroom instruction.

NOTE: The letter and single pages of the booklet may be photocopied but only as many times as you need them for use with individual children, small groups, or an entire class. Reproduction of this material for an entire school system or for sale is strictly forbidden.

You may order copies of the booklets from The Center for Applied Research in Education. The minimum quantity is twenty.

Please note that the booklets contain activities and an award not presented in the booklet for Grades 4-6 since they are more appropriate for the grades PreK-K and Grades 1-3 volumes of the Social Skills Curriculum Activities Library. Nonetheless, the activities and award should prove useful to parents with children of varying ages in their household.

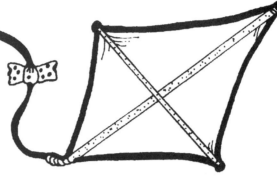

Dear Family:

In our classroom we are learning how to get along with each other; how to deal with our feelings; and how to deal with peer pressure. These are some of the things we are learning in our classroom lessons called Social Skills Training. We not only learn about these Social Skills, but also get a chance to practice those skills through role playing. After we role play the Social Skills in class, we discuss our role playing and practice the skills in school, at play and at home.

Your child,

We are Flying High

Partners
in
Social Skills

A Family Affair

RUTH WELTMANN BEGUN, Editor
The Society for Prevention of Violence
with
The Center for Applied Research in Education

Acknowledgments

The Founders, Trustees, Members, Friends of the Society for Prevention of Violence (SPV), and many Foundations and Corporations sponsored the writing of this social skills training booklet, "Partners in Social Skills: A Family Affair." The objective of the booklet is to acquaint the family with social-skills training and how it can be used to resolve conflicts and to improve the behavior, attitude, and responsibility of the children and other family members. The booklet will help the family reinforce Social-Skills Training being taught in schools and can also be used by the family to teach social skills to preschool children.

Credit for writing the booklet belongs to a group of teachers from the Cleveland (Ohio) Public Schools who worked under the guidance of Ruth Weltmann Begun, then Executive Director of SPV. All participants utilized their expertise and considered many variations of instructional approaches and ideas until a format for the publication was agreed upon.

Introduction

"Partners in Social Skills: A Family Affair" is a Social Skills Training resource guide to be used in a family setting. Social Skills Training helps a child to gain valuable skills such as self-esteem, self-control, respect for other persons, and responsibility for one's own actions. Such skills are very important for good family relationships, solid learning in school, and success all through life.

Some schools now offer Social Skills Training in their classrooms. For many children this supports what they are already learning at home. For many others, school is where they start to learn such skills. Many families today have single parents, or have two parents who both work, or have stepparents due to divorce and remarriage. All these changes put stress on families, and make parenting more challenging than in the past.

Today, the average child watches several hours of television each day, often without a parent or other adult present. TV scenes of violence or other harmful conduct can easily misguide young children.

This guide is designed to help parents in several ways:

(1) To introduce Social Skills Training to parents, and show them how this is already taught in some schools.

(2) To present some Social Skills Training activities that can be done at home.

(3) To encourage parents to apply this training with all of their children, even preschoolers.

(4) To remind parents that, no matter how much they may sometimes doubt it, *they* are the most important teachers in their children's lives.

The love, example, and guidance of parents and other adult family members can indeed make the difference for a child. He or she can learn, with their help, to respect others, make wise decisions, avoid violence, and become a successful and productive citizen as an adult.

Along the way, practicing the Social Skills included here should help the family enjoy a happier and less stressful home life.

Table of Contents

R = reproducible

Cover Page 1

Copyright and Acknowledgments 2

Introduction 3

Table of Contents 4

Our Family Social Skills Training Checklist 5R

Helpful Hints for Using This Book 6

Be a Role Model for Your Child 7

Family Activity Page 8R

Fourteen Selected Social Skills with Suggested Activities 9

    1. Giving Compliments

    2. Asking Permission

    3. Disciplinary Strategies

    4. Respect for Others

    5. Using Self-Control

    6. Improving Self-Image

    7. Expressing Feelings

    8. Accepting Consequences

    9. Reacting to Failure

   10. Setting Goals

   11. Dealing With Prejudice

   12. Dealing With Anger

   13. Dealing With Peer Pressure

   14. Problem Solving

Family Activity Page 17R

"Mirror, Mirror" Poem 18R

Family Activity Page, Certificate 19

Family Time—Group Discussions 20

What Makes You Happy? 21R

Parent-Teacher Communication 22

Our Family Social Skills Training Checklist 23R

Guidelines for Caring Parents 24

OUR FAMILY SOCIAL SKILLS TRAINING CHECKLIST

Directions: Please fill out this checklist as a family before starting to read this book. Answer the way your family really feels by filling in the faces. There are no right or wrong answers.

This will help your family understand the need to practice Social Skills Training in your home.

Almost Always	Sometimes	Almost Never
🙂	😐	🙁

© 1996 by Society for Prevention of Violence

		Almost Always	Sometimes	Almost Never
1.	Do we understand and follow when directions are given?	🙂	😐	🙁
2.	Do we know and follow the rules in our home?	🙂	😐	🙁
3.	Do we listen to adults in authority?	🙂	😐	🙁
4.	Do we finish our household jobs?	🙂	😐	🙁
5.	Do we take our finished homework to school the next day?	🙂	😐	🙁
6.	Do we finish our housework even when others are not doing their share?	🙂	😐	🙁
7.	Do we keep busy and quiet when waiting for our parent's attention?	🙂	😐	🙁
8.	Do we find something quiet and helpful to do when we have free time?	🙂	😐	🙁
9.	Do we deal with anger in a way that won't hurt others?	🙂	😐	🙁
10.	Do we stay in control when somebody teases us?	🙂	😐	🙁
11.	Do we think of ways other than fighting to handle our problems?	🙂	😐	🙁
12.	Do we avoid fighting when someone threatens or hits us?	🙂	😐	🙁
13.	Do we accept the consequences when we do something we shouldn't?	🙂	😐	🙁
14.	Do we tell others that we like something nice about them or do something nice for them?	🙂	😐	🙁
15.	Do we say and do nice things for ourselves when we have earned it?	🙂	😐	🙁

HELPFUL HINTS FOR USING THIS BOOK

1. Set aside quiet time and space.

2. Involve all family members.

3. Discussions should be friendly, positive, and open.

4. Listen to each member's comments.

5. Criticism should be done in a positive and peaceful way.

6. All family members should work on being good role models.

BE A ROLE MODEL FOR YOUR CHILD

- Let your child see you read. Visit the library with your child on a regular basis. At home, provide a quiet, well-lighted space for your child to study and read.

- Don't leave your children alone for long periods of time. Let your child know where and how to reach you. Leave your child with a happy feeling.

- Use kind and supportive words with your child. Unkind words can hurt as much as, or even more than physical punishment.

- When resolving disputes or conflicts in the family, do your best to stay calm and in control of yourself.

- Beginning with yourself, make all family members responsible for keeping themselves and the house clean.

- Show your child how to "just say no" by your *own* saying no to drugs and other harmful activities.

- Remember that your child is learning from you, not only when you are telling him or her what to do, but *all* the time, by your example.

Toot Your Own Horn

Write or draw five things you can do well at home, at work, at school or at play.

FOURTEEN SELECTED SOCIAL SKILLS

The following pages contain fourteen selected Social Skills that have been taken from the "Social Skills Curriculum Activities Library" published by The Center for Applied Research in Education. Each skill is followed by skill activities. It is suggested that these activities can be done with all the family to develop the skill.

FAMILY SOCIAL SKILLS

Skill No. 1:   Giving Compliments:

Compliments mean saying something nice that makes someone else feel good.

Do these skill activities with your family:

1. Select someone to give a compliment.
2. Think of a compliment that is pleasing and truthful.
3. Say the compliment in a pleasant way.

Skill No. 2:   Asking Permission:

Permission means giving consent.

Do these skill activities with your family:

1. Ask if you may borrow something.
2. Do not take the item if the answer is no.
3. If given permission, be careful with the item and return it in good condition.
4. Say "thank you."

Skill No. 3: Disciplinary Strategies:

Discipline is training and conduct that develops self-control.

Do these skill activities with your family:

1. Develop rules and consequences for family members.

2. Encourage all members to follow the rules.

3. Evaluate and change the rules when needed.

Skill No. 4: Respect for Others:

Respect means to be kind and courteous to others.

Do these skill activities with your family:

1. Use the words "may I" when asking someone for something.

2. Use "please" and "thank you" when asking and receiving help.

3. Practice using these words often.

Skill No. 5:   Using Self-Control:

Self-control is remaining calm under stress and excitement.

Do these skill activities with your family:

1. Stop and think about the situation that was causing stress to you and made you excited.
2. Count to ten while trying to remain calm.
3. Decide what you will do next.
4. Do it in a peaceful manner.

Skill No. 6:   Improving Self-Image:

Self-image is how you see yourself.

Do these skill activities with your family:

1. Think of something you like about yourself.
2. Share it with your family members.
3. Discuss more ways you are special.

Skill No. 7:   Expressing Feelings:

Some feeling words are: happy, sad, angry, embarrassed, depressed, proud, guilty, frustrated, and many more.

Do these skill activities with your family:

1. Listen to the tone of voice, watch facial expressions and body gestures to understand the feelings in a message.
2. Ask the speaker if you understood his or her feelings correctly.

Skill No. 8:   Accepting Consequences:

Accepting the results of one's own actions without complaining.

Do these skill activities with your family:

1. Decide if what you did was wrong.

2. Admit what you did was wrong.

3. Try to explain why you did it.

4. Accept the punishment without complaint.

Skill No. 9:   Reacting to Failure:

Failure is an unsuccessful attempt to achieve a goal.

Do these skill activities with your family:

1. Discuss what it means to fail.

2. Decide why you failed.

3. Accept the failure.

4. Make a new plan to avoid making any similar mistakes.

Skill No. 10: Setting Goals:

Goals are plans of action which can be achieved.

Do these skill activities with your family:

1. Think about things that need to be done at home or school.
2. Choose a goal and decide how it can be reached.
3. Reward yourself when you have reached your goal.

Skill No. 11: Dealing With Prejudice:

Prejudice is caused because of differences existing between people which are not acceptable to you.

Do these skill activities with your family:

1. Discuss individual physical differences.
2. Discuss likenesses.
3. Treat everyone equally and with respect.
4. Discuss positive qualities and include everyone in your activities.

Skill No. 12: Dealing With Anger:

Everyone gets angry but anger must be resolved in a peaceful, verbal and nonphysical manner.

Do these skill activities with your family:

1. Stop and think about how you feel.
2. Think of nonthreatening ways to handle your anger.
3. Choose an action that will resolve the conflict.
4. If there is no other choice, walk away.

Skill No. 13: Dealing With Peer Pressure:

Peer Pressure means that pressure is being strongly forced on you by friends, to do something you might or might not want to do. You might decide that what they want you to do is right or wrong.

> We all have friends that we adore
> And that they like us we are sure
> We know they're friends because they care
> We know they're friends because they're fair
> Then there are others that are fakes
> We must watch out for our own sakes
> They'll try to get us to do much wrong
> So with these people we don't belong
> Say no to things you see are bad
> And for yourself you'll be glad
> Friends won't ask us to misbehave
> If you say no, we'll rave and rave.

After reading the poem do these skill activities with your family:

1. Decide if what your friends want you to do is right or wrong. If it seems wrong, consider the consequences. Don't join activities which hurt, damage others, or yourself. If caught you might be imprisoned and penalized. Say "NO" to drugs, alcohol, and early sex. They will harm you.

2. Make a decision you can live with.

3. Think of other activities the group could participate in that are acceptable.

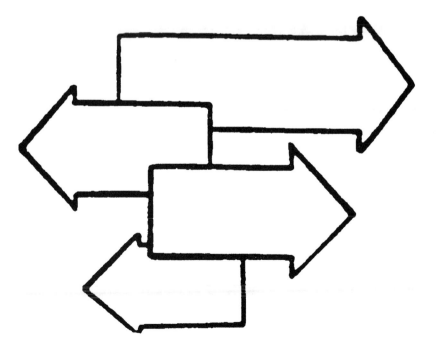

Skill No. 14: Problem Solving:

There are many ways to solve a problem and make a decision. All possibilities should be considered to find the best solution.

Do these skill activities with your family:

1. State the problem and list ways it can be solved.

2. Select and try one of the choices.

3. If it does not work try another solution until you find the best one.

FAMILY ACTIVITY PAGE

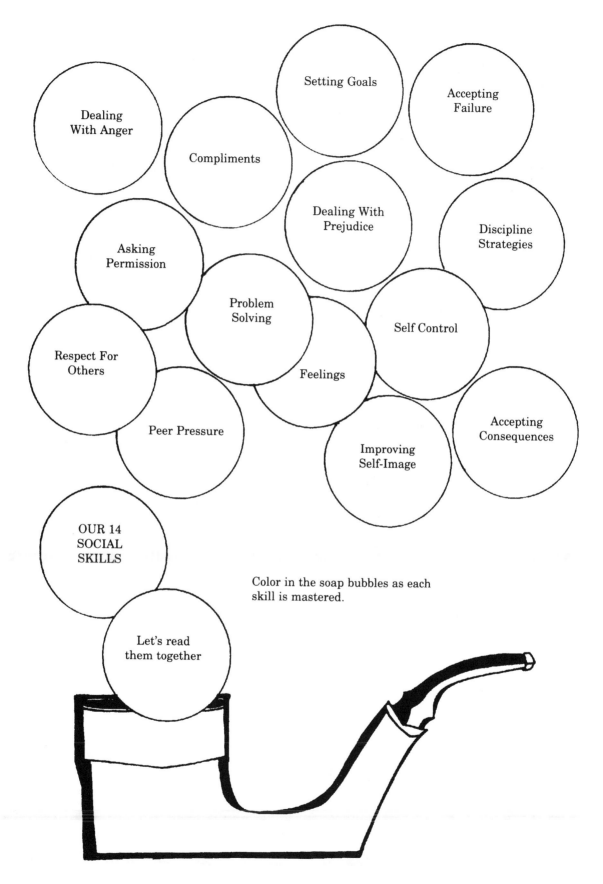

Setting Goals

Accepting Failure

Dealing With Anger

Compliments

Dealing With Prejudice

Discipline Strategies

Asking Permission

Problem Solving

Self Control

Respect For Others

Feelings

Peer Pressure

Accepting Consequences

Improving Self-Image

OUR 14 SOCIAL SKILLS

Color in the soap bubbles as each skill is mastered.

Let's read them together

"MIRROR, MIRROR" POEM

Read the poem. Think of someone to compliment. Draw his/her picture, and write the compliment underneath.

Mirror, mirror on the wall
Give a compliment, and that's not all
Make it nice and make it kind
A deserving person is not hard to find.

KEEP MOVING
YOU ARE LOOKING GOOD!

NAME:

SKILLS:

DATE:

Use this certificate to reward family members for proper use of social skills.

FAMILY TIME—GROUP DISCUSSIONS

Directions to Family: Please set aside ten to fifteen minutes daily to discuss the following questions with family members. During the family discussion be sure to listen to each other. Every family member should be encouraged to give input. Refer to the Social Skills listed in this book.

1. What Social Skills did you learn today?

2. What Social Skills did you use today?

3. What Social Skills did we use within our home?

4. What Social Skills did you use in solving a personal conflict?

5. Did you use courtesy words like "please" and "thank you" when requesting and receiving assistance?

6. What did you do today that made you feel proud?

7. What assignments including household chores did you complete today?

8. Were there any consequences that were difficult for you to accept?

9. How did you show respect for someone today?

10. Did you compliment someone today? How did this make you feel? How did this make the other person feel?

11. Which Social Skill will be our goal to work on tomorrow?

WHAT MAKES YOU HAPPY?

Directions to Family: It is suggested that all family members take part in this activity. Each member may list or draw three things that make them happy. (You may want to use additional paper.)

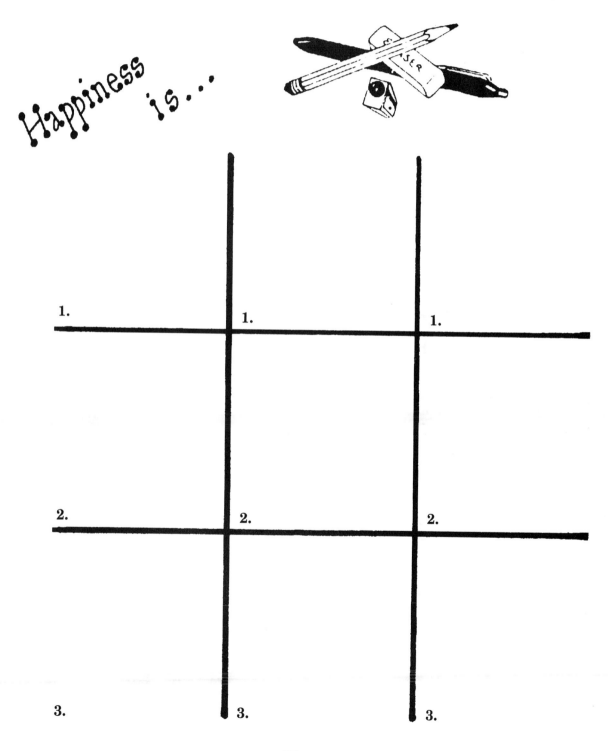

Happiness is...

1.   1.   1.

2.   2.   2.

3.   3.   3.

PARENT-TEACHER COMMUNICATION

1. Make appointments to visit your child's teacher or teachers.

2. Ask about any new changes in the curriculum.

3. Become a part of the PTA and other school-related groups.

4. Get to know your principal.

5. Become aware of Parent Conference days, and become aware of your child's progress.

6. Learn about the community resources that can be of service to you and your family.

7. Feel free to spend time in your child's classroom to see how Social Skills Training is taught.

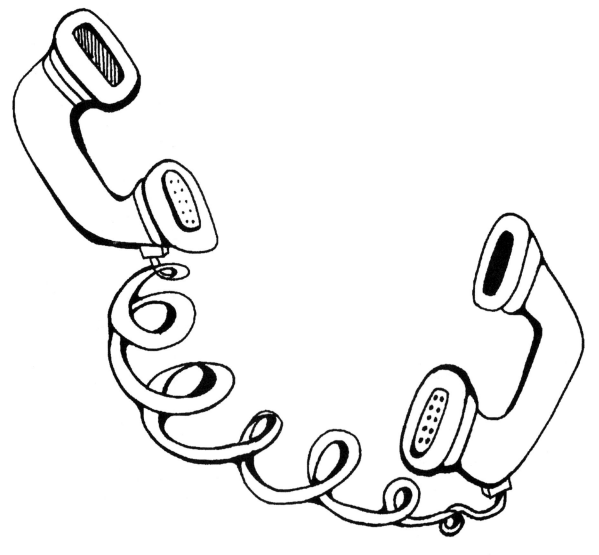

OUR FAMILY SOCIAL SKILLS TRAINING CHECKLIST

Directions: Please fill out this reaction sheet as a family, when you have completed this book.

This may be used to help your family better understand what Social Skills need to be reinforced within the home.

		Almost Always	Sometimes	Almost Never
		☺	😐	☹

		Almost Always	Sometimes	Almost Never
1.	Do we understand and follow when directions are given?	☺	😐	☹
2.	Do we know and follow the rules in our home?	☺	😐	☹
3.	Do we listen to adults in authority?	☺	😐	☹
4.	Do we finish our household jobs?	☺	😐	☹
5.	Do we take our finished homework to school the next day?	☺	😐	☹
6.	Do we finish our housework even when others are not doing their share?	☺	😐	☹
7.	Do we keep busy and quiet when waiting for our parent's attention?	☺	😐	☹
8.	Do we find something quiet and helpful to do when we have free time?	☺	😐	☹
9.	Do we deal with anger in a way that won't hurt others?	☺	😐	☹
10.	Do we stay in control when somebody teases us?	☺	😐	☹
11.	Do we think of ways other than fighting to handle our problems?	☺	😐	☹
12.	Do we avoid fighting when someone threatens or hits us?	☺	😐	☹
13.	Do we accept the consequences when we do something we shouldn't?	☺	😐	☹
14.	Do we tell others that we like something nice about them or do something nice for them?	☺	😐	☹
15.	Do we say and do nice things for ourselves when we have earned it?	☺	😐	☹

GUIDELINES FOR CARING PARENTS

I. How your children learn to act depends on what they are taught—and YOU are their most important teacher.

II. Your children will learn more from watching what you do than from listening to what you say to do.

III. Remember that you were once a child, and treat your children with patience and understanding.

IV. Be fair, be consistent, and respect your children as you would have them respect you.

V. Stay close to your children, but give them room to learn from their own experiences and to think for themselves.

VI. Show your children things in life that are beautiful, and show that you appreciate these things.

VII. Love your children with all your heart, your mind and your strength, and everything else will follow.